Introduction

Problem solving develops not only a student's math skills but also their logical thinking and abstract thinking skills. The students need to be able to recognize the important elements in the problem, identify key words that tell which math operation(s) should be done, and know which problem-solving strategy is the best choice to answer the question. The student must also compare the answer(s) to the information presented in the problem. Does the answer make sense? Does it answer all parts of the question?

About this Book

The variety of math problems in *Daily Warm-Ups: Problem-Solving Math* will provide students with enough problem-solving practice to introduce your math period every day for an entire school year. For each warm-up, allow 10 to 15 minutes for reading, interpreting, and solving the problems before you correct them as a class.

Students can work on the problems in this book independently, in groups, or as a whole class. Decide which approach works best for your students, based on their math skill levels and reading competence.

The book is divided into two sections. The first section of the book introduces five specific problem-solving strategies with math problems that are not directly addressed to a specific operation or concept. The math strategies are as follows: Drawing a Diagram, Creating a Table, Acting It Out or Using Concrete Materials, Guessing and Checking, and Looking for a Pattern. (See pages 8–12 for examples of math problems to which these types of strategies apply.) The second section of the book contains more traditional problems in operations, numeration, geometry, measurement, data analysis, probability, and algebra. The general math area and focus addressed in each warm-up is noted at the top of each page.

These activities can be used in a variety of ways, but they were designed to be introductory warm-ups for each math period. The 250 warm-ups are individually numbered and should be used in any order according to your main math lessons. Choose warm-ups that cover concepts previously taught so that the warm-up can serve as a review.

Standards

The math problems in this book have been correlated to the National Council of Teachers of Mathematics (NCTM) standards. See the correlation chart on pages 5–7. You will find the NCTM standards and the Common Core State Standards and expectations along with the warm-up numbers to which they relate. As the NCTM math standards make clear, problem solving is the critical component in math instruction. It is the component that makes general operations knowledge both essential and useful. Problem solving is the basic element in the concept of math as a method of communication.

Introduction (cont.)

Daily Warm-Ups, Section 1

The 50 warm-ups in this section follow one of five key problem-solving strategies. Each of these pages is set up the same way, allowing students to quickly become familiar with the expectations of the problems. The answers to the problems in this section have been provided along with explanations of the thinking process behind solving each one. (See pages 163–170 for Section 1's answers.)

Math strategy requested to solve the problem

Student's final answer(s) should be written here (if line is given)

Student's brief explanation of steps taken to solve problem (encourage use of math vocabulary)

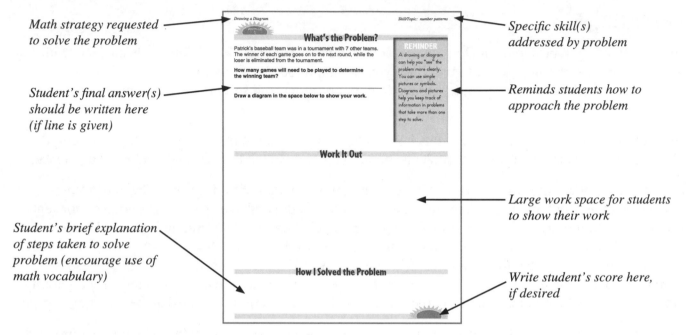

Specific skill(s) addressed by problem

Reminds students how to approach the problem

Large work space for students to show their work

Write student's score here, if desired

Daily Warm-Ups, Section 2

The 200 warm-ups in this section are divided into five math areas: Numbers and Operations, Geometry, Measurement, Data Analysis and Probability, and Algebra. Each of these pages has two warm-ups on the page. The two warm-ups relate to each other in some way. Warm-ups may be separated and given to students independently. Encourage students to apply math strategies as they solve the problems in this section.

Math area and focus

Student's final answer(s) should be written here (if lines are given)

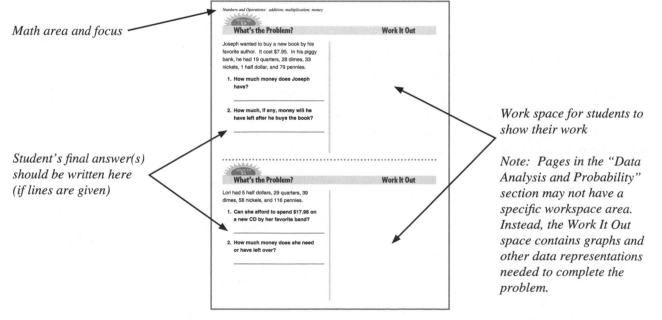

Work space for students to show their work

Note: Pages in the "Data Analysis and Probability" section may not have a specific workspace area. Instead, the Work It Out space contains graphs and other data representations needed to complete the problem.

Correlation to Standards

The following chart lists the National Council of Teachers of Mathematics (NCTM) standards and expectations for grades 3–5. Reprinted with permission from *Principles and Standards for School Mathematics*. (Copyright 2000 by the National Council of Teachers of Mathematics. All rights reserved.) Visit *http://www.teachercreated. com/standards/* for correlations to the Common Core State Standards.

Standards and Expectations	Warm-Up Numbers
NUMBER AND OPERATIONS	
Understand numbers, ways of representing numbers, relationships among numbers, and number systems	
• Understand the place-value structure of the base-ten number system and be able to represent and compare whole numbers and decimals	18, 36–38, 41, 45–47, 49, 51–54, 61–62, 74, 77–78, 83–84
• Recognize equivalent representations for the same number and generate them by decomposing and composing numbers	23, 36–38, 44–45, 53–54, 61–62, 73–74
• Develop understanding of fractions as parts of unit wholes, as parts of a collection, as locations on number lines, and as divisions of whole numbers	34, 57–58, 63–72, 81–82
• Use models, benchmarks, and equivalent forms to judge the size of fractions	57–58, 65–72, 81–82
• Recognize and generate equivalent forms of commonly used fractions, decimals, and percents	34, 37–38, 67–72, 81–82
• Describe classes of numbers according to characteristics such as the nature of their factors	45, 58–59, 85–86
Understand meanings of operations and how they relate to one another	
• Understand various meanings of multiplication and division	15–17, 20, 35, 44, 46, 48, 51, 55–57, 59–60, 73–76
• Understand the effects of multiplying and dividing whole numbers	12, 15–16, 30, 35, 51–52, 55–60, 73–76, 79–80
• Identify and use relationships between operations, such as division as the inverse of multiplication, to solve problems	12, 17
Compute fluently and make reasonable estimates	
• Develop fluency with basic number combinations for multiplication and division and use these combinations to mentally compute related problems, such as 30 × 50	32, 85–90
• Develop fluency in adding, subtracting, multiplying, and dividing whole numbers	30, 73–80, 83–88, 105–108
• Develop and use strategies to estimate the results of whole-number computations and to judge the reasonableness of such results	23, 30, 37–38, 48, 53–54, 85–86, 89–90
• Develop and use strategies to estimate computations involving fractions and decimals in situations relevant to students' experience	32, 38, 79–80
• Select appropriate methods and tools for computing with whole numbers from among mental computation, estimation, calculators, and paper and pencil according to the context and nature of the computation and use the selected method or tools	53–54, 79–80, 85–86

Standards are listed with the permission of the National Council of Teachers of Mathematics (NCTM). NCTM does not endorse the content or validity of these alignments.

Standards and Expectations	Warm-Up Numbers
GEOMETRY **Analyze characteristics and properties of two- and three-dimensional geometric shapes and develop mathematical arguments about geometric**	
• Identify, compare, and analyze attributes of two- and three-dimensional shapes and develop vocabulary to describe the attributes	29, 31, 91–104, 109–114, 117–118, 121–128
• Classify two- and three-dimensional shapes according to their properties and develop definitions of classes of shapes such as triangles and pyramids	9, 29, 91–99, 105–106, 109–114, 117–122, 155–156
• Investigate, describe, and reason about the results of subdividing, combining, and transforming shapes	7, 9, 29, 97–98, 111–114, 117–126
• Make and test conjectures about geometric properties and relationships and develop logical arguments to justify conclusions	31, 97–99, 106–116, 119–124
Specify locations and describe spatial relationships using coordinate geometry and other representational systems	
• Describe location and movement using common language and geometric vocabulary	33, 109–110, 115–116, 123–128, 155–156
Use visualization, spatial reasoning, and geometric modeling to solve problems	
• Build and draw geometric objects	29, 97–98, 109–110, 119–120, 123–126, 153–156
• Create and describe mental images of objects, patterns, and paths	31, 33, 153–154
• Use geometric models to solve problems in other areas of mathematics, such as number and measurement	21, 29, 115–116, 157–158
• Recognize geometric ideas and relationships and apply them to other disciplines and to problems that arise in the classroom or in everyday life	31, 103–104, 115–116, 157–158
MEASUREMENT **Understand measurable attributes of objects and the units, systems, and processes of measurement**	
• Understand such attributes as length, area, weight, volume, and size of angle and select the appropriate type of unit for measuring each attribute	131–148, 157–158
• Understand the need for measuring with standard units and become familiar with standard units in the customary and metric systems	131–138, 141–144, 157–158
• Understand that measurements are approximations and how differences in units affect precision	131–144
Apply appropriate techniques, tools, and formulas to determine measurements	
• Select and apply appropriate standard units and tools to measure length, area, volume, weight, time, temperature, and the size of angles	139–140, 147–152, 157–158, 163–164, 167–170
• Develop, understand, and use formulas to find the area of rectangles and related triangles and parallelograms	115–116, 119–124, 127–130, 147–150
• Develop strategies to determine the surface areas and volumes of rectangular solids	115–116, 127–130, 145–146, 149–150

Standards and Expectations	Warm-Up Numbers
DATA ANALYSIS AND PROBABILITY	
Formulate questions that can be addressed with data and collect, organize, and display relevant data to answer them	
• Design investigations to address a question and consider how data-collection methods affect the nature of the data set	160, 162, 173–174, 205–206, 209–210
• Collect data using observations, surveys, and experiments	160, 162, 171–172, 189–190, 195–206, 209–210
• Represent data using tables and graphs such as line plots, bar graphs, and line graphs	24–27, 42–43, 157–162, 165–168, 175–176, 189–190, 195–206
Select and use appropriate statistical methods to analyze data	
• Describe the shape and important features of a set of data and compare related data sets, with an emphasis on how the data are distributed	1–2, 5–6, 8, 13, 18–19, 26–27, 39–40, 44, 49–50, 159–160, 165–174, 189–190
• Use measures of center, focusing on the median, and understand what each does and does not indicate about the data set	177–178, 181–182
• Compare different representations of the same data and evaluate how well each representation shows important aspects of the data	25, 28, 165–166, 187–188
Develop and evaluate inferences and predictions that are based on data	
• Propose and justify conclusions and predictions that are based on data and design studies to further investigate the conclusions or predictions	175–176, 183–188, 191–194
Understand and apply basic concepts of probability	
• Predict the probability of outcomes of simple experiments and test the predictions	20–21, 179–180, 185–186, 191–194, 207–208
ALGEBRA	
Understand patterns, relations, and functions	
• Describe, extend, and make generalizations about geometric and numeric patterns	40, 45–48, 215–218, 221–222, 225–238
• Represent patterns and functions, using words, tables, and graphs	211–222, 233–238
Represent and analyze mathematical situations and structures using algebraic symbols	
• Identify such properties as commutativity, associativity, and distributivity and use them to compute with whole numbers	223–232
• Represent the idea of a variable as an unknown quantity using a letter or a symbol	211–220, 223–225, 227, 229, 248
• Express mathematical relationships using equations	211–218, 223–224, 229–246
Use mathematical models to represent and understand quantitative relationships	
• Model problem situations with objects and use representations such as graphs, tables, and equations to draw conclusions	3–4, 10–11, 13–14, 244, 248
Analyze change in various contexts	
• Investigate how a change in one variable relates to a change in a second variable	11, 13–14, 215–216, 239–242

Examples of Strategies

Drawing a Diagram

A drawing or diagram can help you "see" the problem more clearly. You can use simple pictures or symbols. Diagrams and pictures help you keep track of information in problems that take more than one step to solve.

Example 1

What's the Problem?

Katie's ball bounces half the distance of any height from which it is dropped. She dropped the ball from the top of a building that is 64 feet high.

How high will the ball bounce after the sixth bounce?

Work It Out

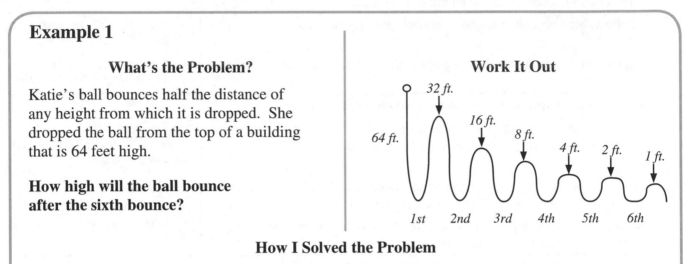

How I Solved the Problem

To solve the problem, a student might draw a diagram of the ball dropping from a height of 64 feet. The student would then draw each bounce half as high as the previous bounce. Each bounce height would be calculated and labeled. After 6 bounces, the answer will be found.

Example 2

What's the Problem?

Five boys played on the Oak Elementary School basketball team. Xavier scored 17 points in the last game, which were 4 more than Nate scored. Theo scored 7 more than Xavier and 3 more than Owen. Josh scored one less than Nate.

How many points did each boy score?

How many total points did the team score?

Work It Out

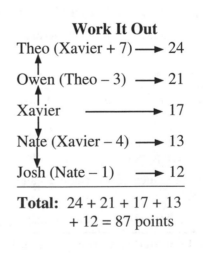

Theo (Xavier + 7) ⟶ 24

Owen (Theo – 3) ⟶ 21

Xavier ⟶ 17

Nate (Xavier – 4) ⟶ 13

Josh (Nate – 1) ⟶ 12

Total: 24 + 21 + 17 + 13 + 12 = 87 points

How I Solved the Problem

To solve the problem, a student would begin with what he or she knows, which is Xavier's point total. The student would then add and/or subtract to find the other players' totals. Drawing a diagram (like the one shown in the "Work It Out" section) would help a student keep the information straight as new pieces of data were added.

Creating a Table

Creating a table helps you organize the information.

Follow these steps:

1. Work in order and list all combinations.
2. Keep one item the same while others change.
3. Fill in any gaps.
4. Record the solution so it is easy to understand.

Example 1

What's the Problem?

Cassandra spent her whole vacation collecting shells on a beach. She noticed that for every 7 shells she collected, 3 were perfectly preserved and unbroken and 4 were damaged. In one week, she collected 42 shells.

How many of the shells were unbroken?

How many shells were damaged?

Work It Out

Total	Unbroken	Damaged
7	3	4
14	6	8
21	9	12
28	12	16
35	15	20
42	18	24

How I Solved the Problem

To solve the problem, a student would use the information given to fill in the first row of a chart. If the student followed the pattern and continued the chart, he or she would arrive at the answer.

Example 2

What's the Problem?

Carla has a blue hat and a red hat. She also has 3 scarves (purple, gray, and black).

How many different combinations of hats and scarves can she wear without repeating the same combination?

Create a table to show your work.

Work It Out

	Hat	Scarf
1.	blue	purple
2.	blue	gray
3.	blue	black
4.	red	purple
5.	red	gray
6.	red	black

How I Solved the Problem

To solve the problem, a student would create a chart listing all combinations in order. By keeping one item the same (the hat) until all combinations are listed, the student can keep the information straight.

Acting It Out or Using Concrete Materials

Sometimes a problem is hard to visualize or to solve. Use real objects to create a model or use people (or objects) to act out the problem and its solution.

By acting it out, talking through the problem, or using objects to represent parts of the problem, you can "see" its solution better.

Example 1

What's the Problem?

There are 5 players on Tina's volleyball team. Each player likes to high-five each other player after each point.

How many high-fives are there in all after each point.

Work It Out

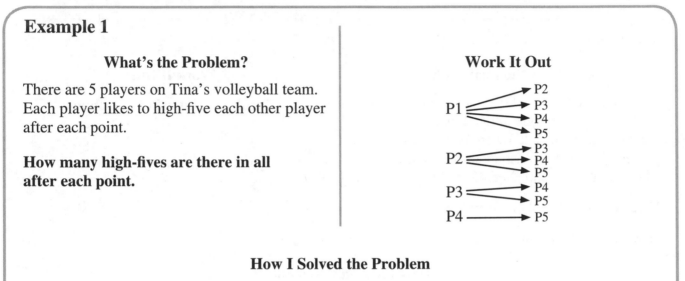

How I Solved the Problem

To solve the problem, a student might use other people to literally re-create (or act out) the problem

Example 2

What's the Problem?

Four girls had a puddle-jumping contest after a long rainy day. Ana jumped 4 inches farther than Grace and 2 inches farther than Mia. Kat jumped 23 inches, which was 5 inches farther than Ana jumped.

In what order did the girls finish?

How many inches did each girl jump?

Work It Out

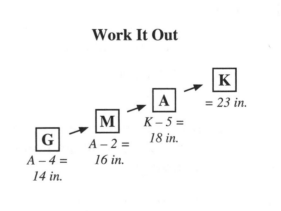

How I Solved the Problem

To solve the problem, a student might use objects or other people to represent each of the girls. The student would then act out the problem by moving the people or objects according to the information given.

Guessing and Checking

Guessing and checking helps you find reasonable guesses to solve a problem. For each guess, look at the important information presented in the problem. Check the guess against the information. Base the next guess on the previous result to see if it was too large or too small. Repeat the steps until the problem is solved. (Recording your guesses and results in a table helps, too!)

Example 1

What's the Problem?

Uncle Joey is 18 years old. His nephews, Mark and Ross, are 5 and 3 years old.

How old will Joey be when his nephews combined ages are the same as his?

Work It Out

	Mark	Ross	Joey
Guess 1	9	7	22
Guess 2	11	9	24
Guess 3	13	11	26
Guess 4	15	13	28

How I Solved the Problem

To solve the problem, a student might first create a table. He or she might then add 2 years to each age to see the results. The student might continue to add a few years each time until the answer is revealed.

Example 2

What's the Problem?

Milo has a lot of pets—22 in all. He has 3 more birds than he does dogs. He has 5 fewer cats than he does birds. He has 7 more fish than he does cats.

How many of each kind of animal does he have?

Work It Out

	Dogs	Birds	Cats	Fish	Total
Guess 1	2	5	0	7	14
Guess 2	3	6	1	8	18
Guess 3	4	7	2	9	22

How I Solved the Problem

To solve the problem, a student might use a table to record guesses. The student could begin by guessing the number of dogs and filling in the chart using the information given.

Looking for a Pattern

Looking for patterns makes it easier to predict what comes next. In a problem, study any number patterns to see how the numbers change from one number to the next. For example, to find the rule for the pattern 2, 4, 8, 16, study how 2 and 4, 4 and 8, etc., are related. You will see that each number is double (2 times) the number before it.

Example 1

What's the Problem?

Pedro was learning to bounce a soccer ball on his knee without letting it hit the ground. On the first day, he could only do it twice, but on the second day, he did it 5 times. Then he did it 7 times on the third day and 10 times on the fourth day.

Following this pattern, how often will Pedro be able to do it on the seventh day?

Work It Out

Day	Bounces
1	2
2	5
3	7
4	10
5	12
6	15
7	17

How I Solved the Problem

To solve the problem, a student might use a table to record the data and decode the pattern. The pattern here was "+2" every odd day and "+3" every even day.

Example 1

What's the Problem?

Nick's new computer company is taking off. They sold 3 computers in the first week and 6 computers in the second week. Amazingly, this pattern continued, and so the company sold 48 computers in the fifth week!

What is the pattern of sales Nick's company is following.

Work It Out

Week	Computer Sold
1	3
2	6
3	12
4	24
5	48

How I Solved the Problem

To solve the problem, a student might use a table to record the data, leaving the missing information blank. The student might then try filling in different data until the pattern is decoded.

Warm-Up 1

What's the Problem?

Patrick's baseball team was in a tournament with 7 other teams. The winner of each game goes on to the next round, while the loser is eliminated from the tournament.

How many games will need to be played to determine the winning team?

_____

Draw a diagram in the space below to show your work.

REMINDER

A drawing or diagram can help you "see" the problem more clearly. You can use simple pictures or symbols. Diagrams and pictures help you keep track of information in problems that take more than one step to solve.

Work It Out

How I Solved the Problem

Warm-Up 2

What's the Problem?

Five students ran in their school's Field Day competition. Chris beat Allie by 7 yards, but he was 2 yards behind Elena. Derrick finished 4 yards behind Allie but 2 yards ahead of Bart.

In what order did the five students finish?

_____

_____

_____

_____

_____

Draw a diagram in the space below to show your work.

Work It Out

How I Solved the Problem

Warm-Up 3

What's the Problem?

Four fourth-grade baseball teams finished their season. The Angels had 5 more wins than the Giants. The Red Sox had 3 more wins than the Angels but 2 wins less than the Yankees.

In what order did the teams finish?

1st: _____   3rd: _____

2nd: _____   4th: _____

If the Giants had 9 wins, how many wins did each team have?

_____

_____

_____

_____

Draw a diagram in the space below to show your work.

REMINDER
A drawing or diagram can help you "see" the problem more clearly. You can use simple pictures or symbols. Diagrams and pictures help you keep track of information in problems that take more than one step to solve.

Work It Out

How I Solved the Problem

Warm-Up 4

What's the Problem?

Four fourth-grade boys ran a race to see who was the fastest runner. Sergio was beaten by Randy, but Estevan was faster than Randy. Jimmy was faster than Estevan.

In what order did the boys finish the race?

_____

_____

_____

_____

Draw a diagram in the space below to show your work.

Work It Out

How I Solved the Problem

Warm-Up
5

What's the Problem?

Four sisters collected seashells on the beach to give to the local museum. Amy collected 13 shells more than Allison. Allison collected 19 shells. Anmol collected 6 shells less than Allison and 4 shells more than Alicia.

How many shells did each girl collect?

_____

_____

_____

_____

How many shells did the sisters collect altogether? _____

Draw a diagram in the space below to show your work.

REMINDER

A drawing or diagram can help you "see" the problem more clearly. You can use simple pictures or symbols. Diagrams and pictures help you keep track of information in problems that take more than one step to solve.

Work It Out

How I Solved the Problem

Warm-Up 6

What's the Problem?

Five brothers built a sand fort. Albert carried 11 pails of sand to build the fort. James brought 7 more pails than Albert but 6 pails fewer than Joshua. Nathan brought 3 more pails than Joshua. Justin brought 1 pail less than Albert.

How many pails did each brother bring?

_____

_____

_____

_____

_____

How many pails did they bring altogether? _____

Draw a diagram in the space below to show your work.

Work It Out

How I Solved the Problem

Warm-Up
7

What's the Problem?

Elaine helped decorate her grandma's house this summer. She was in charge of creating a pattern for the kitchen floor. She was given pieces of blue tile that looked like this:

How could Elaine use four tiles to make a larger equilateral triangle?

How could she use four tiles to make a parallelogram?

How could she use six tiles to make a hexagon?

Draw a diagram in the space below to show your work.

REMINDER

A drawing or diagram can help you "see" the problem more clearly. You can use simple pictures or symbols. Diagrams and pictures help you keep track of information in problems that take more than one step to solve.

Work It Out

How I Solved the Problem

Warm-Up
8

What's the Problem?

The fourth graders had a Valentine's Day party. Four girls counted the number of hearts on their cards. Victoria had 12 more hearts than Valerie and 13 less than Violet. Vicki had 7 more hearts than Violet.

Who had the most hearts?

_____

Who had the least number of hearts?

_____

Draw a diagram in the space below to show your work.

REMINDER

A drawing or diagram can help you "see" the problem more clearly. You can use simple pictures or symbols. Diagrams and pictures help you keep track of information in problems that take more than one step to solve.

Work It Out

How I Solved the Problem

**Warm-Up
9**

What's the Problem?

Paul baked a batch of birthday brownies in a square pan. He wanted to divide it equally among the 4 people at the party.

Show how Paul can cut the whole pan of brownies so that each person gets one equal portion? (Find three ways.)

Right after Paul cut the brownies in fourths, 4 more people arrived at the party. What can Paul do to cut the brownies so that each person now at the party gets one equal portion?

Use the space below to draw diagrams to answer the questions.

REMINDER

A drawing or diagram can help you "see" the problem more clearly. You can use simple pictures or symbols. Diagrams and pictures help you keep track of information in problems that take more than one step to solve.

Work It Out

How I Solved the Problem

Warm-Up 10

What's the Problem?

REMINDER

A drawing or diagram can help you "see" the problem more clearly. You can use simple pictures or symbols. Diagrams and pictures help you keep track of information in problems that take more than one step to solve.

Six sea scouts cleared the litter from their local beach last Saturday. Jason collected 19 bags of litter. Joshua collected 15 more bags than Jason and 1 less bag than Arlene. Brandon collected 9 more bags than Arlene and 3 more than April. Keith collected 5 less than Joshua.

How many bags did each scout collect?

_____   _____

_____   _____

_____   _____

Draw a diagram in the space below to show your work.

Work It Out

How I Solved the Problem

What's the Problem?

Justin placed 1 nickel in a jar on Sunday. He put 3 nickels in the jar on Monday. He placed 9 in the jar on Tuesday.

Following the same pattern, how many nickels will Justin put in the jar on Friday?

_____

Complete the table below to answer the question.

REMINDER

Creating a table helps you organize the information.
Follow these steps:
1. Work in order and list all combinations.
2. Keep one item the same while others change.
3. Fill in any gaps.
4. Record the solution so it is easy to understand.

Work It Out

Day of the Week	Number of Nickels
Sunday	1
Monday	3
Tuesday	9

How I Solved the Problem

Warm-Up
12

What's the Problem?

Adrian went to the school carnival. For every 7 tickets he bought, he received 3 free tickets. He bought 56 tickets.

How many free tickets did he receive?

_____

How many tickets did he have altogether?

_____

Complete the table below to answer the questions.

REMINDER

Creating a table helps you organize the information.
Follow these steps:
1. Work in order and list all combinations.
2. Keep one item the same while others change.
3. Fill in any gaps.
4. Record the solution so it is easy to understand.

Work It Out

Bought Tickets	Free Tickets
7	3

How I Solved the Problem

What's the Problem?

Steven started a swimming program in the pool after school. He swam 2 laps the first day, and he swam 3 laps the next day. He swam 5 laps the following day, 8 laps the day after that, and 12 laps on the fifth day of his swimming program.

Following the same pattern, on what day will he swim 23 laps?

_____

On what day will he swim 47 laps?

_____

Complete the table below to answer the questions.

Work It Out

Day	Number of Laps
1st day	2
2nd day	3
3rd day	5

How I Solved the Problem

What's the Problem?

April started an exercise program. On the first day, she exercised for 1 minute. On the second day, she exercised for 3 minutes. On the third day, she exercised for 7 minutes. On the fourth day, she exercised for 15 minutes.

Following the same pattern, how many minutes will she exercise on each of the next two days?

_____

_____

Complete the table below to answer the questions.

Work It Out

Day	Number of Minutes
1st day	1
2nd day	3
3rd day	7

How I Solved the Problem

Warm-Up 15

What's the Problem?

The Whizzer Wheel at the amusement park has 12 cars. It holds 8 people in each car. However, Jeremy noticed that 5 out of 8 seats in each car were empty.

How many seats were empty?

_____

How many seats were occupied?

_____

Complete the table below to answer the questions.

REMINDER

Creating a table helps you organize the information.
Follow these steps:
1. Work in order and list all combinations.
2. Keep one item the same while others change.
3. Fill in any gaps.
4. Record the solution so it is easy to understand.

Work It Out

Car	Empty Seats	Occupied Seats
1st car	5	
Total		

How I Solved the Problem

What's the Problem?

Richard picked apples at an orchard during the summer. He noticed that only 5 out of every 9 apples were perfect enough to sell. The rest would be used to make cider. He picked 108 apples.

How many apples were perfect?

_____

Create a table in the space below to show your work.

REMINDER

Creating a table helps you organize the information.
Follow these steps:
1. Work in order and list all combinations.
2. Keep one item the same while others change.
3. Fill in any gaps.
4. Record the solution so it is easy to understand.

Work It Out

How I Solved the Problem

**Warm-Up
17**

What's the Problem?

In his teacher's classroom library, Mike saw that 7 out of every 10 fiction books were adventure stories. There were 140 fiction books in the library.

How many books were adventure stories?

_____

Create a table in the space below to show your work.

Work It Out

How I Solved the Problem

What's the Problem?

Elizabeth likes to fly model wooden gliders. Out of every 7 gliders that she owns, 5 can stay airborne for a minute or longer. She has 12 gliders that do not stay airborne for a minute.

How many of her gliders do stay airborne?

_____

Create a table in the space below to show your work.

Work It Out

How I Solved the Problem

Warm-Up
19

What's the Problem?

Aaron and Erin took a survey of favorite treats with 10 of their fourth-grade classmates. They discovered that 5 children preferred ice cream sundaes, 3 preferred cake, and 2 preferred candy.

If this pattern remained when they surveyed 40 students, how many would prefer each dessert?

_____

Create a table in the space below to show your work.

REMINDER

Creating a table helps you organize the information.
Follow these steps:
1. Work in order and list all combinations.
2. Keep one item the same while others change.
3. Fill in any gaps.
4. Record the solution so it is easy to understand.

Work It Out

How I Solved the Problem

Warm-Up 20

What's the Problem?

Jeanette has a red blouse, a blue blouse, and a yellow blouse. She has white shorts and black shorts.

How many different combinations of blouses and shorts can she wear without repeating the same combination?

Create a table in the space below to show your work.

REMINDER

Creating a table helps you organize the information.

Follow these steps:

1. Work in order and list all combinations.
2. Keep one item the same while others change.
3. Fill in any gaps.
4. Record the solution so it is easy to understand.

Work It Out

How I Solved the Problem

What's the Problem?

Farmer MacDonald is taking a chicken; a pail of corn; and a large, hungry dog to market. He needs to cross a river in a very small boat that will only hold himself and one other passenger or item. He cannot leave the chicken with the corn or the chicken will eat the corn. He cannot leave the dog with the chicken, because the dog will eat the chicken.

How can he get them all safely across the river?

_____

_____

_____

How many trips will he have to make across the river?

_____

If you wish, use the space below to work out the solution to the problem.

REMINDER

Sometimes a problem is hard to visualize or to solve. Use real objects to create a model or use people (or objects) to act out the problem and its solution.

By acting it out, talking through the problem, or using objects to represent parts of the problem, you can "see" its solution better.

Work It Out

How I Solved the Problem

What's the Problem?

There are 5 different coins hidden under a napkin on a table. They are a penny, a dime, a quarter, a half dollar, and a silver dollar. The penny is to the right of the silver dollar. The quarter is to the left of the dime and to the right of the penny. The half dollar is last.

Put the coins in order from left to right.

_____

If you wish, use the space below to work out the solution to the problem.

REMINDER

Sometimes a problem is hard to visualize or to solve. Use real objects to create a model or use people (or objects) to act out the problem and its solution.

By acting it out, talking through the problem, or using objects to represent parts of the problem, you can "see" its solution better.

Work It Out

How I Solved the Problem

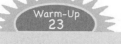
Warm-Up 23

What's the Problem?

A blue card is worth 10 points in a board game. A black card is worth half as much as a blue card. A red card is worth twice as much as a blue card.

How many points does a player have if he has 3 black cards, 3 blue cards and 3 red cards?

_____

If you wish, use the space below to work out the solution to the problem.

Work It Out

How I Solved the Problem

What's the Problem?

Jill was swimming in the ocean 75 yards from shore. The waves were pushing very hard against her. She decided to swim to shore. She could only swim 20 yards toward shore before she had to rest. While she rested, the waves pushed her back 5 yards during each rest.

If this pattern continued, how many times did Jill have to swim and rest until she made it safely to shore?

_____

If you wish, use the space below to work out the solution to the problem.

Work It Out

How I Solved the Problem

Warm-Up 25

What's the Problem?

There are 4 students in Amy's ballet class. Each student must shake hands with every other student before class begins.

How many handshakes will there be in all?

_____

If you wish, use the space below to work out the solution to the problem.

REMINDER

Sometimes a problem is hard to visualize or to solve. Use real objects to create a model or use people (or objects) to act out the problem and its solution.

By acting it out, talking through the problem, or using objects to represent parts of the problem, you can "see" its solution better.

Work It Out

How I Solved the Problem

What's the Problem?

Carrie, Bobby, Irene, and Joey tossed a beanbag back. Each friend did that once with each other friend.

How many total times was the beanbag tossed?

_____

If you wish, use the space below to work out the solution to the problem.

Work It Out

How I Solved the Problem

What's the Problem?

Five snails were speeding along a wet, smooth plastic board in a race toward the finish line. Slippery Sam was ahead of Happy Harry but behind Dashing Dan. Fearless Freddy was ahead of Dashing Dan but behind Muddy Max.

List the order in which the snails were racing.

_____

_____

_____

_____

If you wish, use the space below to work out the solution to the problem.

Work It Out

How I Solved the Problem

What's the Problem?

Joey has 9 marbles, which look exactly alike. The weight of 8 of the marbles is exactly the same. The weight of the last marble is slightly heavier. It is very valuable.

How can Joey find the heavier valuable marble in just two weighings on an equal arm balance?

_____

_____

_____

_____

_____

If you wish, use the space below to work out the solution to the problem.

REMINDER

Sometimes a problem is hard to visualize or to solve. Use real objects to create a model or use people (or objects) to act out the problem and its solution.

By acting it out, talking through the problem, or using objects to represent parts of the problem, you can "see" its solution better.

Work It Out

How I Solved the Problem

What's the Problem?

Mr. Smith gave Kenny's class a tough assignment. He took them outside to the playground and asked them to use a 12-foot piece of rope to make as many geometric shapes with sides as they could. For each shape, the measurement of each side had to be an equal, whole number of feet. Kenny was able to make 5 shapes.

What 5 shapes did Kenny make from the 12-foot piece of rope?

_____   _____

_____   _____

_____

Draw a picture in the space provided to illustrate each yarn shape. Label each side of each figure with its correct measurement.

REMINDER

Sometimes a problem is hard to visualize or to solve. Use real objects to create a model or use people (or objects) to act out the problem and its solution.

By acting it out, talking through the problem, or using objects to represent parts of the problem, you can "see" its solution better.

Work It Out

How I Solved the Problem

What's the Problem?

Five friends decided to read one book as a team. Jamie read the first 80 pages. Jennifer read the next 40 pages.

If this pattern continued, how many pages did each of the next three students read?

_____

_____

_____

If this pattern was followed and the book was finished by the fifth person, how many pages long was the book?

_____

If you wish, use the space below to work out the solution to the problem.

Work It Out

How I Solved the Problem

Warm-Up 31

What's the Problem?

Jordan swims laps every day in a rectangular swimming pool. The perimeter of the pool is 300 feet. The length of the pool is 10 feet longer than the width.

What is the length of the pool? What is the width?

_____

_____

Use the chart below to solve the problem.

Work It Out

Length	Width	Perimeter

How I Solved the Problem

Warm-Up 32

What's the Problem?

Adrianne bought an ice cream cone at the county fair that cost $3.50. She paid the cashier in quarters and dimes. She used 7 more dimes than she used quarters.

How many dimes did Adrianne use?

_____

How many quarters did she pay with?

_____

Use the chart below to solve the problem.

REMINDER

Guessing and checking helps you find reasonable guesses to solve a problem. For each guess, look at the important information presented in the problem. Check the guess against the information. Base the next guess on the previous result to see if it was too large or too small. Repeat the steps until the problem is solved. (Recording your guesses and results in a table helps, too!)

Work It Out

Quarters	Dimes	Total Money

How I Solved the Problem

What's the Problem?

In the fourth-grade ball box, there are 3 more softballs than kickballs. There are 2 fewer footballs than kickballs. There are 4 more volleyballs than softballs.

Put the balls in order from the greatest number to the least.

_____

_____

How many balls of each kind are there if the total number of balls equals 28?

_____

_____

_____

_____

Use the space below to show your work.

Work It Out

How I Solved the Problem

What's the Problem?

Derrick's dad is 30 years old. Derrick is 8.

How old will Derrick be when he is half as old as his father?

_____

Use the space below to show your work.

Work It Out

How I Solved the Problem

What's the Problem?

Carry's family went to a minor league baseball game. Tickets were $5 for children and $8 for adults. Her father spent $72 for tickets.

How many children's tickets and how many adult tickets did he buy? (Hint: He bought at least one ticket at each price.)

_____

_____

Use the space below to show your work.

Work It Out

How I Solved the Problem

What's the Problem?

Jeremy made this problem for his dad to solve. Each letter can represent only one number. The D always equals the same one-digit number. The same is true for the E and the F.

$$DDD$$

$$+ EEE$$

$$\overline{FFF}$$

Use the space below to solve the problem for his father. Find 10 different answers.

Work It Out

How I Solved the Problem

Warm-Up 37

What's the Problem?

Jessica wanted to find how many different combinations of quarters, dimes, and nickels she could use to make $0.50.

Can you help her find 10 combinations?

_____   _____

_____   _____

_____   _____

_____   _____

_____   _____

Use the space below to show your work.

REMINDER

Guessing and checking helps you find reasonable guesses to solve a problem. For each guess, look at the important information presented in the problem. Check the guess against the information. Base the next guess on the previous result to see if it was too large or too small. Repeat the steps until the problem is solved. (Recording your guesses and results in a table helps, too!)

Work It Out

How I Solved the Problem

Warm-Up 38

What's the Problem?

Tiffany bought a mouse at the pet store for $2.65. She paid in nickels and quarters from her piggy bank. She used 11 more nickels than quarters.

How many nickels did she use?

_____

How many quarters did she use?

_____

Use the space below to show your work.

Work It Out

How I Solved the Problem

Warm-Up 39

What's the Problem?

Sharon picked 65 ripe apples in a 5-day period. Each day she picked 4 more apples than the day before.

How many apples did she pick each day?

_____

_____

_____

_____

_____

Use the space below to show your work.

REMINDER

Guessing and checking helps you find reasonable guesses to solve a problem. For each guess, look at the important information presented in the problem. Check the guess against the information. Base the next guess on the previous result to see if it was too large or too small. Repeat the steps until the problem is solved. (Recording your guesses and results in a table helps, too!)

Work It Out

How I Solved the Problem

What's the Problem?

Sherrie is 9 and her mother is 29.

How old will Sherrie be when she is exactly half as old as her mother?

_____

Use the space below to show your work.

Work It Out

How I Solved the Problem

Warm-Up 41

What's the Problem?

Lauren read 3 books in September. She read 6 books in October. She read 9 books in November.

What is the pattern Lauren is following?

_____

_____

_____

If she keeps up the same pattern, how many books will she read in February?

_____

Complete the chart below to solve the problem.

Work It Out

Month	Books Read
September	3
October	6

How I Solved the Problem

What's the Problem?

Jamie collects baseball cards. He collected 3 in February, 5 in March, 8 in April, and 12 in May.

What is the pattern?

_____

_____

Following this pattern, how many cards will he collect in June, July, August, and September?

_____

_____

How many will he have collected altogether by October 31?

_____

Complete the chart below to solve the problem.

REMINDER

Looking for patterns makes it easier to predict what comes next. In a problem, study any number patterns to see how the numbers change from one number to the next. For example, to find the rule for the pattern 2, 4, 8, 16, study how 2 and 4, 4 and 8, etc., are related. You will see that each number is double (2 times) the number before it.

Work It Out

Month	Books Collected
February	3
March	5
April	8

How I Solved the Problem

Warm-Up 43

What's the Problem?

Andrea is getting in shape for a summer bikeathon. She rode her bike 1 mile every day the first week. The second week she rode 2 miles every day. She rode 4 miles every day during the third week and 8 miles every day during the fourth.

What is the pattern?

_____

_____

If she continued in this pattern, how many miles did she ride daily during the sixth week?

_____

Complete the chart below to solve the problem.

REMINDER

Looking for patterns makes it easier to predict what comes next. In a problem, study any number patterns to see how the numbers change from one number to the next. For example, to find the rule for the pattern 2, 4, 8, 16, study how 2 and 4, 4 and 8, etc., are related. You will see that each number is double (2 times) the number before it.

Work It Out

Week	Miles
1	1
2	2
3	4

How I Solved the Problem

What's the Problem?

Kimberly met 2 new friends in January when she joined a social network on the Internet. She met 8 new friends in February. In March, she met 32 new friends. This pattern continued, and she met over 500 new friends in May.

What is the pattern?

_____

_____

_____

How many friends will Kimberly meet in June?

_____

Complete the chart below to solve the problem.

Work It Out

Month	Friends Met
January	2
February	8
March	32

How I Solved the Problem

What's the Problem?

Sharon began collecting stickers of all types. On the first day, she collected and pasted 6 stickers into a scrapbook. On the second day, she collected 9 stickers for a total of 15 stickers. Each day, she collected and pasted 3 more stickers into her book than she did the day before.

How many total stickers did Sharon have after 8 days?

_____

Complete the chart below to solve the problem.

Work It Out

Day	Stickers	Total
1	6	6
2	9	15
3		

How I Solved the Problem

What's the Problem?

Mitchell keeps a penny jar. He collects pennies from the sidewalk, under sofas, and every place he can find them. The first week he put 1 penny in the jar. The second week he put 2 pennies in the jar. The third week he added 4 pennies. The fourth week he added 8 pennies.

What is the pattern?

_____

_____

_____

Following this pattern, on what week would he add more than 1,000 pennies to his jar?

_____

Complete the chart below to solve the problem.

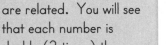

REMINDER

Looking for patterns makes it easier to predict what comes next. In a problem, study any number patterns to see how the numbers change from one number to the next. For example, to find the rule for the pattern 2, 4, 8, 16, study how 2 and 4, 4 and 8, etc., are related. You will see that each number is double (2 times) the number before it.

Work It Out

Week	Pennies Added
1st	1
2nd	2
3rd	4

How I Solved the Problem

Warm-Up
47

What's the Problem?

Annalee joined a chorus because she loved to sing. She knew 3 songs the first week. The second week, she knew 4 songs. After 3 weeks she knew 6 songs. She knew 9 songs after 4 weeks.

What is the pattern?

_____

_____

_____

How many songs did she know after 8 weeks?

_____

In the space below, draw a chart to help you find the pattern.

REMINDER

Looking for patterns makes it easier to predict what comes next. In a problem, study any number patterns to see how the numbers change from one number to the next. For example, to find the rule for the pattern 2, 4, 8, 16, study how 2 and 4, 4 and 8, etc., are related. You will see that each number is double (2 times) the number before it.

Work It Out

How I Solved the Problem

Warm-Up
48

What's the Problem?

Harvey had a box of 96 wrapped chocolate candies. He gave away 48 candies to friends the first day. He gave away 24 candies to friends the second day.

What is the pattern?

_____

_____

_____

Following this pattern, on what day will Harvey have only 3 candies left?

_____

In the space below, draw a chart to help you find the pattern.

REMINDER

Looking for patterns makes it easier to predict what comes next. In a problem, study any number patterns to see how the numbers change from one number to the next. For example, to find the rule for the pattern 2, 4, 8, 16, study how 2 and 4, 4 and 8, etc., are related. You will see that each number is double (2 times) the number before it.

Work It Out

How I Solved the Problem

Warm-Up 49

What's the Problem?

Alyse had a huge birthday party. When the doorbell rang the first time, her best friend entered. The next time, 3 people entered. On the next ring, 5 people entered. On the fourth ring, 7 people entered.

What is the pattern?

_____

_____

Following this pattern, how many people will enter on the 10th ring?

_____

How many total people will be at the party on the 10th ring?

_____

In the space below, draw a chart to help you find the pattern.

REMINDER

Looking for patterns makes it easier to predict what comes next. In a problem, study any number patterns to see how the numbers change from one number to the next. For example, to find the rule for the pattern 2, 4, 8, 16, study how 2 and 4, 4 and 8, etc., are related. You will see that each number is double (2 times) the number before it.

Work It Out

How I Solved the Problem

What's the Problem?

Nathan measured the distance between the rings of an old tree stump in millimeters. He noticed a pattern starting to form. Here were his measurements from the center of the stump to the bark:

1, 2, 2, 3, 3, 3, 4, __, __, __, __, __, __, __, __, __

What is the pattern?

_____

_____

_____

What are the next 9 numbers in the pattern? Fill in the spaces on the pattern above.

If you wish, use the space below to work on the solution to this problem.

REMINDER

Looking for patterns makes it easier to predict what comes next. In a problem, study any number patterns to see how the numbers change from one number to the next. For example, to find the rule for the pattern 2, 4, 8, 16, study how 2 and 4, 4 and 8, etc., are related. You will see that each number is double (2 times) the number before it.

Work It Out

How I Solved the Problem

Warm-Up 51

What's the Problem?

Work It Out

Megan's 16-year-old brother bought a used car. He has to pay $150 a month for 36 months.

How much will the car cost him altogether?

_____

Warm-Up 52

What's the Problem?

Work It Out

Megan's brother has to pay a yearly registration fee of $88.50 and buy car insurance, which will cost him $365.64 per year.

How much does her brother have to pay altogether for insurance and registration each year?

_____

Warm-Up 53

What's the Problem?

Work It Out

Joseph wanted to buy a new book by his favorite author. It cost $7.95. In his piggy bank, he had 19 quarters, 28 dimes, 33 nickels, 1 half dollar, and 79 pennies.

1. **How much money does Joseph have?**

   _____

2. **How much, if any, money will he have left after he buys the book?**

   _____

Warm-Up 54

What's the Problem?

Work It Out

Lori had 5 half dollars, 29 quarters, 39 dimes, 58 nickels, and 116 pennies.

1. **Can she afford to spend $17.98 on a new CD by her favorite band?**

   _____

2. **How much money does she need or have left over?**

   _____

Warm-Up 55

What's the Problem?

Work It Out

Andrea and Alexis are twins. They were given 40 quarters, 30 dimes, 20 nickels, and 10 pennies by their favorite aunt. They divided the money in half.

How much money, in dollars and cents, did each twin receive?

_____

Warm-Up 56

What's the Problem?

Work It Out

Jake, John, and Joey are triplets. They received 120 dollar bills, 60 half dollars, and 36 quarters from their favorite uncle. They split the money evenly.

How much money, in dollars and cents, did they each receive?

_____

Warm-Up 57

What's the Problem?   Work It Out

Jody's neighbor has a huge garden with many vegetables and fruits. In one week, he gave Jody's family 2 dozen apples, 1 dozen tomatoes, $1\frac{1}{2}$ dozen potatoes, $\frac{1}{2}$ dozen limes, and 3 dozen lemons.

How many fruits and vegetables did he give Jody's family altogether?

_____

Warm-Up 58

What's the Problem?   Work It Out

Elaine picked 6 dozen apples from her trees. She also gathered $2\frac{1}{2}$ dozen squash, 4 dozen potatoes, $\frac{1}{2}$ dozen tomatoes, and 1 dozen plums.

How many fruits and vegetables did she gather in all?

_____

Warm-Up 59

What's the Problem?

Work It Out

Brandon collects stamps and keeps them in a special book. He keeps 9 stamps on each page.

How many pages will he need for 108 stamps?

_____

Warm-Up 60

What's the Problem?

Work It Out

Brandon's grandfather sent him a baggie with 342 stamps.

How many pages of 9 stamps will he be able to fill with those stamps?

_____

Warm-Up 61

What's the Problem?

Work It Out

James played 5 basketball games for his local team. He made 11 shots worth 3 points, 27 shots worth 2 points each, and made 13 foul shots worth 1 point each.

How many points did he score over the five games?

Warm-Up 62

What's the Problem?

Work It Out

James wanted to compute his scoring average over 9 games. He scored these points in his 9 games: 23 points, 10 points, 12 points, 14 points, 6 points, 20 points, 10 points, 17 points, and 5 points.

What was his average number of points per game?

Warm-Up 63

What's the Problem?

Work It Out

Reggie's mother bought an "everything on it" pizza for Reggie and his brother, Ronnie, to share. Reggie ate $\frac{1}{4}$ of the pizza, and his brother ate $\frac{3}{8}$ of the pizza.

How much did they eat altogether?

_____

Warm-Up 64

What's the Problem?

Work It Out

For dessert, Ronnie ate $\frac{1}{3}$ of a chocolate cake, and Reggie ate $\frac{1}{2}$ of the cake.

How much of the cake did they eat in all?

_____

What's the Problem?   Work It Out

At a pizza party, James ate $\frac{1}{2}$ of a pizza. Elizabeth ate $\frac{1}{3}$ of a pizza. Elaine ate $\frac{3}{6}$ of a pizza. Rudy ate $\frac{4}{8}$ of a pizza. Carlos ate $\frac{5}{8}$ of a pizza.

Which children ate the same amount of pizza as James?

_____

Warm-Up 66

What's the Problem?   Work It Out

Jonathan completed $\frac{3}{4}$ of a page of math problems. Patrick completed $\frac{7}{8}$ of the same page.

1. **Who completed more problems?**

_____

2. **How much more did that person complete?**

_____

Warm-Up 67

What's the Problem?

Work It Out

Thomas went to bat 10 times for his summer league team, the Angels, in one series against the Rays. He got 6 hits and struck out 4 times.

Which fraction and decimal pair best expresses his hitting? (Circle the letter next to the correct answer.)

A. $\frac{6}{4}$ and 0.40

B. $\frac{4}{10}$ and 0.60

C. $\frac{6}{10}$ and 0.60

D. $\frac{4}{6}$ and 0.66

Warm-Up 68

What's the Problem?

Work It Out

Thomas got 12 hits in 16 times at bat during a week of baseball games played in the summer.

Which fraction and decimal pair best expresses his hitting in lowest terms? (Circle the letter next to the correct answer.)

A. $\frac{3}{4}$ and 0.60

B. $\frac{1}{2}$ and 0.75

C. $\frac{3}{4}$ and 0.75

D. $\frac{1}{2}$ and 0.60

Warm-Up 69

What's the Problem?

Work It Out

Norma received a bag of her favorite wrapped candies for her birthday. It contained 100 pieces. She and her friends ate 25 of the candies in one afternoon.

Which fraction and decimal pair best expresses the part of the candy that Norma and her friends ate? (Circle the letter next to the correct answer.)

   A. $\frac{25}{75}$ and 0.33

   B. $\frac{3}{4}$ and 0.75

   C. $\frac{1}{4}$ and 0.14

   D. $\frac{1}{4}$ and 0.25

• •

Warm-Up 70

What's the Problem?

Work It Out

Norma and her sister, Sheila, ate 10 chocolates from a box of 50 in one afternoon.

Which two fractions express the number of candies they ate? (Circle the letter next to the correct answer.)

   A. $\frac{10}{50} = 1/2$

   B. $\frac{10}{50} = 1/5$

   C. $\frac{40}{50} = 1/2$

   D. $\frac{10}{50} = 5/1$

Warm-Up 71

What's the Problem?

Work It Out

Jared found 3 quarters underneath his bed.

What fractional part of a dollar did he find? Write it as two different equivalent fractions.

_____

_____

Warm-Up 72

What's the Problem?

Work It Out

Jolene took 1 quarter, 2 dimes, and 3 nickels out of her coin jar.

What fractional part of a dollar did she take? Write the answer with two fractions that equal each other.

_____

_____

Warm-Up
73

What's the Problem?

Work It Out

The 88 fourth graders in Oak Elementary School are going on a field trip to the zoo by car. Each automobile can take only 4 children.

How many cars are needed?

_____

Warm-Up
74

What's the Problem?

Work It Out

All of the students in Rachel Carson Elementary School are going on a field trip to Ocean World Aquarium. There are 66 kindergarteners, 74 first-graders, 80 second-graders, 91 third-graders, 63 fourth-graders, 57 fifth-graders, and 66 sixth-graders.

1. **How many students are going on the trip?**

    _____

2. **If each bus can seat a maximum of 60 students, how many buses will be needed to take all of the students?**

    _____

Numbers and Operations: multiplication; days in a month

Warm-Up 75

What's the Problem?   **Work It Out**

The fourth graders in Miss Wilson's room read 20 pages from a book of their choice every night, including weekends.

How many pages did each child read during the month of November?

_____

Warm-Up 76

What's the Problem?   **Work It Out**

Miss Wilson has 32 students in her classroom, and all of them completed their reading assignments in January. Each read 20 pages every night, including weekends.

How many pages did the entire class read in January?

_____

Warm-Up
77

What's the Problem?   Work It Out

During a school magazine fundraiser to buy playground equipment, Alan sold 40 subscriptions at $29.95 each.

How much money did he collect?

_____

· ·

Warm-Up
78

What's the Problem?   Work It Out

Alicia sold 16 magazine subscriptions at $9.50 each and 12 subscriptions at $15.85 each.

How much money did she collect in all?

_____

Warm-Up 79

What's the Problem?   **Work It Out**

Kathy sold ice cream sundaes at the school carnival. In one hour, she sold 20 triple-scoop sundaes at $4.95 each and 30 double-scoop sundaes at $3.85.

Which of the following is the best estimate of how much money Kathy collected? (Circle the letter next to the correct answer.)

   A. $150

   B. $300

   C. $220

   D. $280

Warm-Up 80

What's the Problem?   **Work It Out**

Peter sold popcorn and soda at the school carnival. In one hour, he sold 40 bags of popcorn at $1.95 each and 30 bottles of soda at $2.95 each.

Which of the following is the best estimate of how much money Peter collected? (Circle the letter next to the correct answer.)

   A. $200

   B. $270

   C. $80

   D. $170

Warm-Up 81

What's the Problem? Work It Out

Mr. Hendersons's fourth-grade class took a spelling test with 20 hard words. Eleanor got $\frac{3}{4}$ of the words correct.

Which of the following expresses the decimal and percentage equivalent of that fraction? (Circle the letter next to the correct answer.)

A. **0.50 and 50%**

B. **0.25 and 25%**

C. **0.75 and 75%**

D. **1.00 and 100%**

Warm-Up 82

What's the Problem? Work It Out

Kyle took a math test with 10 problems. He got $\frac{9}{10}$ of the problems correct.

Which of the following expresses the decimal and percentage equivalent of that fraction? (Circle the letter next to the correct answer.)

A. **0.10 and 10%**

B. **0.90 and 90%**

C. **0.09 and 9%**

D. **0.75 and 75%**

Warm-Up 83

What's the Problem?

Work It Out

Laura Ingalls Wilder, author of the *Little House* books for children, was born on February 7, 1867. She died on February 10, 1957.

How many years old was Mrs. Wilder when she died?

_____

Warm-Up 84

What's the Problem?

Work It Out

President George Washington was born on February 22, 1732. He died December 14, 1799.

How many years old was Washington when he died?

_____

Warm-Up 85

What's the Problem?   Work It Out

In 2009, The New York Public Library had 5,954,897 books. The Cleveland Public Library had 4,273,222 books.

What is the best estimate of the total number of books held by both libraries? (Circle the letter next to the correct answer.)

A. 6,000,000

B. 9,000,000

C. 10,000,000

D. 2,000,000

Warm-Up 86

What's the Problem?   Work It Out

In 2009, the Library of Congress in Washington, D.C., held 32,124,001 books. The Harvard University Library held 15,826,570 books.

About how many more books were shelved at the Library of Congress? (Circle the letter next to the correct answer.)

A. 48 million

B. 16 million

C. 17 million

D. 16 billion

Warm-Up 87

What's the Problem?

Work It Out

Minnie started her button collection with 10 buttons when she was 6 years old. She now has 1,000 buttons at age 10.

How many times as many buttons does she now have than when she started her collection? (Circle the letter next to the correct answer.)

   A. one million

   B. ten

   C. one hundred

   D. one thousand

Warm-Up 88

What's the Problem?

Work It Out

Minnie wants to collect one million buttons by the time she is 18 years old. She has about 1,000 right now.

How many times as many buttons will she need to collect by time she reaches 18 years old? (Circle the letter next to the correct answer.)

   A. 1,000

   B. 100

   C. 10,000

   D. 100,000

What's the Problem?

Work It Out

At Eddie's summer camp, they served 3 pieces of pizza to each of 144 campers. Each pizza had 12 slices.

How many whole pizzas did the campers eat?

_____

What's the Problem?

Work It Out

During lunch at sports camp, they served 3 pieces of pizza to each of 200 campers. Each pizza had 8 slices.

How many pizzas did it take to feed all 200 campers?

_____

Warm-Up 91

What's the Problem?   Work It Out

George lives in an unusual house. There are no right angles on the outside of the house. There are 3 sides to the house. Two of the sides are the same length.

Which picture could be an outline of his house? (Circle the letter next to the correct answer.)

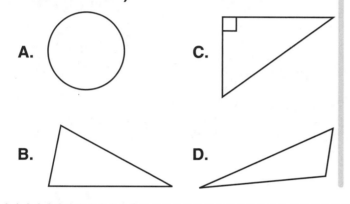

A.

B.

C.

D.

<hr />

Warm-Up 92

What's the Problem?   Work It Out

Donna's family just moved into a house that has 5 equal sides.

What is the name of the shape of her house? (Circle the letter next to the correct answer.)

A. square

B. regular pentagon

C. equilateral triangle

D. hexagon

What's the Problem?

Work It Out

Garrett's room is shaped like a rectangle. The perimeter of the room is 42 feet. The length of one side of his room is 11 feet.

What are the lengths of the other three sides?

_____

_____

_____

Warm-Up
94

What's the Problem?

Work It Out

The kitchen in Garrett's house is shaped like a long rectangle. The perimeter of the kitchen is 80 feet. One short side is 15 feet long.

What are the lengths of the other three sides?

_____

_____

_____

Warm-Up 95

What's the Problem?   Work It Out

Annabelle's famiy just moved into a new house. She can draw 6 straight lines from 6 different corners of the house through the exact center of the house.

Which of the following geometric figures describes the shape of her house? (Circle the letter next to the correct answer.)

   A. square

   B. circle

   C. rectangle

   D. regular hexagon

- -

Warm-Up 96

What's the Problem?   Work It Out

Cody's room has no right angles. It has four sides, and three of the sides are the same length. The fourth side is twice as long as the length of one of the other sides.

Which term best describes the shape of Cody's room? (Circle the letter next to the correct answer.)

   A. triangle

   B. hexagon

   C. trapezoid

   D. rhombus

Warm-Up 97

What's the Problem?

Work It Out

The fourth-grade classroom in Green Valley Elementary School is exactly square like the picture shown here.

Which of the following geometric figures cannot be drawn to fit exactly 4 equal figures into the square? (Circle the letter next to the correct answer.)

A. squares

B. equilateral triangles

C. rectangles

D. circles

- -

Warm-Up 98

What's the Problem?

Work It Out

Joel drew a square like the one pictured to the right.

Which of the following geometric figures can fill up the entire square if it is drawn exactly 8 times equally? (Circle the letter next to the correct answer.)

A. squares

B. equilateral triangles

C. circles

D. isosceles right triangles

Warm-Up 99

What's the Problem?

Work It Out

Peyton loves to play all sports. He has baseballs, tennis balls, footballs, golf balls, kickballs, basketballs, and volleyballs. He knows that in a perfect sphere, the distance through the middle of the sphere from one side to the other is the same between all points.

Which of his balls is *not* a perfect sphere?

_____

Warm-Up 100

What's the Problem?

Work It Out

Planets and moons are all described as spheres.

Describe what features of Earth or other planets would indicate they are *not* perfect spheres.

_____

_____

_____

_____

Warm-Up 101

What's the Problem?

Work It Out

Manny's junior league team plays on a baseball field where each of the four bases is 60 feet apart.

1. **What is the perimeter of the diamond?**

   _____

2. **What is the area of his baseball diamond?**

   _____

Warm-Up 102

What's the Problem?

Work It Out

A major league baseball diamond is 90 feet between each of the four bases.

1. **What is the perimeter of a major league diamond?**

   _____

2. **What is the area of a major league diamond?**

   _____

Warm-Up 103

What's the Problem?   **Work It Out**

Phillip's room is 23 feet long and 17 feet wide.

1. **What is the perimeter of his room?**

   _____

2. **What is the area of his room?**

   _____

Warm-Up 104

What's the Problem?   **Work It Out**

Sandra's room is 24 feet long and 15 feet wide.

1. **What is the perimeter of her room?**

   _____

2. **What is the area of her room?**

   _____

What's the Problem?

Work It Out

Caitlin drew exactly 108 square inches on a piece of paper in the form of a rectangle. One side was 12 inches long.

How wide was the other side?

_____

What's the Problem?

Work It Out

Caitlin invented a rectangular game board that has 120 squares. One side was 12 squares long.

How long is the other side?

_____

Warm-Up 107

What's the Problem?   Work It Out

Troy has used toy building blocks to create a model airport in the shape of a long narrow rectangle. The width of the building is 24 centimeters long. The length is 4 times the width.

What is the total perimeter of the building?

_____

Warm-Up 108

What's the Problem?   Work It Out

Troy designed an airfield that was 200 centimeters long and only 16 centimeters wide.

What is the perimeter of the airfield?

_____

Geometry: area

Warm-Up
109

What's the Problem?

Work It Out

Adrienne designed her own model community using toy blocks. Each block is 2 inches long and 1 inch wide. The base of her community center is 40 inches long and 20 inches wide.

1. **What is the area of the community center's base?**

   _____

2. **How many blocks did she need to make the base?**

   _____

Warm-Up
110

What's the Problem?

Work It Out

As part of her project, Adrienne used blocks to create a model parking lot. The lot is 140 inches long and 70 inches wide.

1. **What is the area of the parking lot?**

   _____

2. **How many blocks 2 inches long and 1 inch wide would be needed to cover the lot?**

   _____

Warm-Up 111

What's the Problem?

Work It Out

Veronica cooked fudge for a birthday party. Each piece was shaped like a cube 1 inch long, 1 inch wide, and 1 inch high.

1. **How many faces were there on each piece of fudge?**

_____

2. **How many points (or vertices) were there on each piece of fudge?**

_____

3. **How many edges were there on each piece of fudge?**

_____

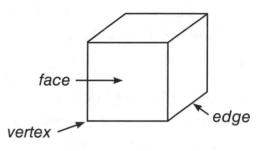

face → *edge*

vertex →

Warm-Up 112

What's the Problem?

Work It Out

Veronica made some special white fudge in a rectangular block 3 inches long, 1 inch wide, and 2 inches high.

How many cubic inches of fudge (pieces 1 inch long, 1 inch wide, and 1 inch high) could be cut from each block of white fudge?

_____

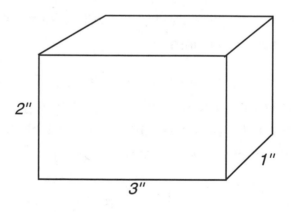

2"   3"   1"

Warm-Up 113

What's the Problem?

Work It Out

Stephen drew the figure shown to the right. It is an equilateral triangle, so it has 3 equal sides.

Which of the following figures can be drawn using 2, 3, or 4 connected equilateral triangles? (Circle the letter next to *each* correct answer.)

    A. parallelogram

    B. equilateral triangle

    C. square

    D. trapezoid

Warm-Up 114

What's the Problem?

Work It Out

Ralph was given the figures below for a math homework assignment.

Which of the following figures can Ralph divide into equilateral triangles using just a ruler and straight lines? (Circle the letter next to *the* correct answer.)

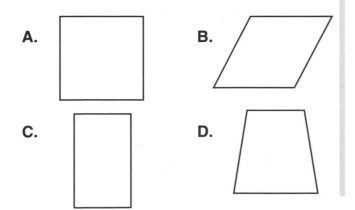

A.

B.

C.

D.

Warm-Up 115

What's the Problem?

Work It Out

Monica cut pieces of a birthday cake that were 4 centimeters long, 4 centimeters wide, and 4 centimeters high.

How many cubic centimeters 1 centimeter long, 1 centimeter wide, and 1 centimeter high would fit into each piece of birthday cake?

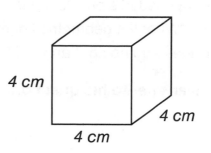

4 cm

4 cm

4 cm

_____

_____

_____

Warm-Up 116

What's the Problem?

Work It Out

Monica's entire birthday cake was 16 centimeters long, 16 centimeters wide, and 4 centimeters high.

1. **How many cubic centimeters were in the entire cake?**

   _____

2. **How many 4-centimeter long by 4-centimeter wide by 4-centimeter high pieces of cake could Monica cut from the cake?**

   _____

What's the Problem?

Work It Out

Alexander posed this puzzle to his friend Matthew: "What flat geometric figure has 4 equal sides and no right angles?"

Draw the answer to his question.

· ·

Warm-Up
118

What's the Problem?

Work It Out

Matthew asked Alexander to solve this puzzle: "What geometric figure can have 3 equal sides, while also having no right angles and 1 longer or 1 shorter side?"

Draw the answer to his puzzle.

Warm-Up 119

What's the Problem?   Work It Out

Walter created a geometric figure that had
a perimeter of 16 inches and an area of
16 square inches.

How long was each side of the figure?

_____

- -

Warm-Up 120

What's the Problem?   Work It Out

Randy looked at the square Walter created.
It had a perimeter of 16 inches and an area
of 16 square inches. Randy wanted to
create a different square that would have the
same number for the perimeter in inches as
the number it had for the area in square
inches.

1. **Will any of the following numbers
   work for Randy's square?**

   36   25   64   4   9   1

   _____

2. **Will any other number less than 100
   (other than 16) work?**

   _____

Warm-Up 121

What's the Problem?

Work It Out

Ricky has a measuring tape 12 inches long.

How many different rectangles, using whole inches, can he make with a perimeter of exactly 12 inches? Draw and label the lengths and widths of each rectangle.

_____

_____

_____

Warm-Up 122

What's the Problem?

Work It Out

Erika has a measuring tape 18 inches long.

1. **How many different rectangles, using whole inches, can she create with perimeters of exactly 18 inches? In the space to the right, draw and label the lengths of each rectangle.**

2. **In the space given, show at least 5 triangles Erica can create with 18-inch perimeters?**

Warm-Up 123

What's the Problem?

Work It Out

Herbert used 36 square-inch pieces to create 5 different rectangles, each with an area of 36 square inches. Each rectangle was a different size.

What are the dimensions (lengths and widths) of each rectangle?

_____

_____

_____

_____

_____

Warm-Up 124

What's the Problem?

Work It Out

Herbert's sister, Michelle, used 48 square-inch pieces to create 5 different rectangles, each with an area of 48 square inches. Each rectangle was a different size.

What are the dimensions (lengths and widths) of each rectangle?

_____

_____

_____

_____

_____

What's the Problem?

Work It Out

Serena sliced a tennis ball into 2 equal parts through the center. She looked at one half of her ball.

Which parts of the ball represent the radius, the circumference, and the diameter? Label the parts on the drawing to the right.

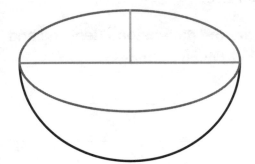

- -

Warm-Up 126

What's the Problem?

Work It Out

Draw a circle in the blank space to the right. Label the circumference of the circle. Next, draw a straight line through the exact center of the circle. Label this line. Then, draw a straight line from the outside of the circle to the center of the circle and label that line.

1. **Which labeled part of the circle is exactly twice as long as another?**

   _____

2. **Using paper, string, or any other flexible object, measure which part of the circle is about 3 times as long as the line through the center of the circle.**

   _____

What's the Problem?

Work It Out

Maricella helped her mother cover a kitchen floor with tiles that were each exactly 1 foot wide and 1 foot long. The kitchen was 22 feet long and 9 feet wide.

How many tiles did she need to cover the floor?

_____

• •

What's the Problem?

Work It Out

Maricella and her mother covered the walls of her room with new wallpaper. Each of the four walls is 10 feet long and 10 feet wide.

1. **How much wallpaper did they need for one wall?**

   _____

2. **How much wallpaper did they need for all four walls?**

   _____

What's the Problem?   Work It Out

Darlene wanted to cover $\frac{1}{2}$ of one wall of her room with shiny, red wallpaper in the shape of a right triangle from the floor to the ceiling. The wall is 12 feet long and 10 feet high.

How much wallpaper would she need to make the triangle covering for her wall?

_____

What's the Problem?   Work It Out

Darlene's teacher, Miss Smith, wanted to cover half of one classroom wall with a right triangle of purple cloth. The wall is 10 feet high and 21 feet long.

How much purple cloth will Miss Smith need for her purple triangle?

_____

Warm-Up 131

What's the Problem?

Work It Out

Joy compared everything she could find to both the centimeter and the inch. She listed all the things in her desk that were about equal in length to the centimeter and those which were about equal to the inch.

|——|

1 centimeter (cm)

|————|

1 inch (in.)

Things About Equal to 1 cm	Things About Equal to 1 inch
fingernail length	top joint of middle finger
pencil top eraser	pink eraser
width of marker top	small pencil sharpener
edge of children's book	edge of paperback novel
edge of spiral binder	edge of math textbook
edge of flash drive	height of computer mouse

Use the measurements at the top of this page to check the things you agree with. Put a "Y" next to those you agree with. Put an "N" next to those you disagree with.

- -

Warm-Up 132

What's the Problem?

Work It Out

Find all of the things in your desk, clothes, shoes, and room that are about 1 centimeter long or wide. Find things that are about 1 inch long or wide.

Record your findings in the table below.

Things About Equal to 1 cm	Things About Equal to 1 inch

What's the Problem?

Work It Out

Ezra knew that a foot was 12 inches long, the length of a ruler. He knew that it was a commonly used unit of measurement. He made a list of things in the classroom that are about 1 foot long.

Items About 1 Foot Long

- the length of this page

- the length of a math book

- his arm from elbow to fingers

- the width of a classmate's back

Use your ruler to estimate the length or width of objects in your classroom.

- -

Warm-Up 134

What's the Problem?

Work It Out

Ezra made a list of objects a little shorter than 1 foot and another list of things that are a little longer than 1 foot.

Add to Ezra's list with other classroom items.

Objects a Little Shorter Than 1 Foot	Objects a Little Longer Than 1 Foot
a child's head	a computer screen (side to side)
a notebook	a computer screen (top to bottom)
a textbook (side to side)	a textbook (top to bottom)

What's the Problem?

A yard is exactly 3 feet long, the length of 3 rulers. A meter is about 3 inches longer than a yard. It is 100 centimeters long.

Patti made a list of items at school and at home that she guessed were about a yard or a meter long. Use a yardstick, a meter stick, or 3 rulers taped together to find which objects on Patti's list were about a yard or meter in length or height.

Look at the chart to the right. Write a "Y" if the object is about a yard or meter in length. Write an "N" if it is not.

Work It Out

Objects About 1 yard or 1 Meter Long or High	Yes or No?
the width and height of a classroom desk	
the height of a student chair	
2 lunch trays side-by-side	
some first-grade children	
the length and width of one piece of sidewalk	
the lowest exercise bar on the playground	

- -

Warm-Up 136

What's the Problem?

Remember, a yard is the length of 3 foot-long rulers, and a meter is about 3 inches longer than a yard.

Measure and list other objects in the classroom or at school that also are about the length of a yard or a meter.

Work It Out

Objects About 1 yard or 1 Meter Long or High	Exact length

Warm-Up 137

What's the Problem?

Work It Out

Nelson made a list of physical features that he thought could be about 1 centimeter and a list he felt could be about 1 inch long.

├───┤
1 centimeter (cm)

Check Nelson's list and make changes, if you disagree. Add features of your own.

├──────┤
1 inch (in.)

Features	Nelson's Measurement	Your Measurement
nose length	1 inch	
height of eye	1 centimeter	
width of eye	1 centimeter	
width of nose	1 centimeter	
fingernail width	1 centimeter	
fingernail length	1 centimeter	
thumb to knuckle	1 inch	
ear length	1 cm	
ear width	1 cm	

Warm-Up 138

What's the Problem?

Work It Out

Now think about the foods you eat. Many—like cereal pieces, macaroni, cut vegetables, fruit pieces, etc.—come in small pieces.

1. **Which pieces of food that you eat are about one centimeter long?**

   _____

   _____

   _____

2. **Which food pieces are about one inch long when you eat them?**

   _____

   _____

   _____

Warm-Up 139

What's the Problem?   Work It Out

Jan measured the approximate length and height of objects at their school with yardsticks and meter sticks. She recorded the approximate measurements.

Use a yardstick or meter stick to measure the objects listed below and others in your classroom, lunchroom, stage, gardens, and playground areas. Compare your results with those collected by Jan.

Objects	Jan's Results	Your Results
small car	4 to 5 yards or meters	
pickup truck	6 yards or meters	
height of the classroom	4 yards or meters	
length of patio	5 to 6 yards or meters	
height of tallest 6th-grader	2 yards or meters	
length of school bus	15 yards or meters	

Warm-Up 140

What's the Problem?   Work It Out

How tall are the objects in your classroom?

For each object listed below, make a guess. Then, using a yardstick or meter stick, take the actual measurement. Add 2 classroom objects of your own to the list.

Object	Estimated Height	Actual Height
your desk		
teacher's desk		
pencil sharpener		
chalkboard or whiteboard		

Warm-Up 141

What's the Problem?   Work It Out

Ann measured the length of her fingers in inches and centimeters.

Measure your fingers and compare them to the measurements Ann recorded.

Ann's fingers (right hand)	Centimeters	Inches
thumb	5 cm	2 in.
forefinger	6 cm	2 in.
middle finger	7 cm	3 in.
ring finger	6 cm	2 in.
little finger	4 cm	1½ in.

Your Fingers (right hand)	Centimeters	Inches
thumb		
forefinger		
middle finger		
ring finger		
little finger		

Warm-Up 142

What's the Problem?   Work It Out

Measure the length of as many small things as you can, including leaves, crayons, markers, school supplies, insects, candy wrappers, and so forth.

Record your information in a chart. Your measurements should be in centimeters and inches.

**Warm-Up
143**

What's the Problem?

Work It Out

Jessica had an empty carton that could hold a quart of liquid and an empty bottle that could hold 1 liter of liquid. She filled the liter bottle with water and then emptied the liter bottle of water into the quart bottle. She discovered that the liter bottle held just a little more liquid than the quart bottle.

What kind of liquids would Jessica or her family buy in quart or liter bottles?

_____

_____

_____

_____

**Warm-Up
144**

What's the Problem?

Work It Out

A gallon holds exactly 4 quarts and a little less than 4 liters.

What kinds of liquids might your family buy by the gallon?

_____

_____

_____

_____

Warm-Up 145

What's the Problem?

Work It Out

Jonathan collected stamps off letters and kept them in a book. Each stamp required 1 square inch of space.

How many stamps could Jonathan fit on the page outlined to the right? Use the space outlined above or a ruler to determine how many stamps would fit.

_____

Warm-Up 146

What's the Problem?

Work It Out

Jonathan wanted to pick pages for his stamp book that could hold the most stamps. Each stamp requires 1 square inch of space. He had three choices of page styles.

1. **How many stamps could Jonathan fit in each of the 3 pages?**

   _____

   _____

   _____

2. **Which page would fit the most stamps?**

   _____

Page B

Page A

Page C

**Warm-Up
147**

What's the Problem?

Work It Out

Kathy wanted her mom to buy her a bedspread decorated with all of her favorite animal characters. The spread is a rectangle that is 6 feet wide and 10 feet long.

1. **Draw a diagram of the spread. Label the length and width.**

2. **What is the perimeter of the spread in feet?**

   _____

3. **What is the area in square feet?**

   _____

**Warm-Up
148**

What's the Problem?

Work It Out

Kathy needs help creating formulas for computing the perimeter and area of a rectangle. Her teacher has told her to use "P" for perimeter, "A" for area, "l" for length, and "w" for width.

1. **Help Kathy create a formula for computing the perimeter of a rectangle.**

   _____

   _____

2. **Help Kathy create a formula for computing the area of a rectangle.**

   _____

What's the Problem?

Work It Out

Cody used a ruler to measure the length of his room that was 12 feet long. The width was 9 feet long. He wanted to pin a long scroll all around the walls of his room. The scroll was 40 feet long.

1. Is the scroll long enough?

_____

2. How many feet long or short is the scroll?

_____

. . . .

Warm-Up 150

What's the Problem?

Work It Out

Cody wanted to decorate the entire ceiling of his 12 ft. x 9 ft. room with a giant space scene on silver and black foil. The piece of foil is 100 square feet in area.

1. What is the area of the ceiling of Cody's room?

_____

2. How many more square feet of foil does he need to cover it?

_____

Warm-Up 151

What's the Problem?

Most temperatures in the United States are measured in degrees Fahrenheit (°F). For instance, water freezes at 32°F and boils at 212°F. Most people have a body temperature of 98.6°F.

Look at this thermometer reading:

1. **Name the temperature in degrees F.**

   _____

2. **What climate or part of day might have been going on during that temperature?**

   _____

   _____

Work It Out

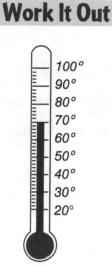

Warm-Up 152

What's the Problem?

For each of the following questions, circle the letter next to the correct answer.

1. **Which of these temperatures would you most likely expect at the beach?**

   A. 40°F   C. 20°F

   B. 90°F   D. 0°F

2. **Which of the following temperatures would you expect on a skiing trip?**

   A. 90°F   C. 120°F

   B. 10°F   D. 70°F

3. **Which of the following temperatures would you expect to find at noon in an African desert in the summer?**

   A. 10°F   C. 120°F

   B. 0°F   D. 50°F

Work It Out

Warm-Up 153

What's the Problem?

Work It Out

Phillip wanted to create these 4 basic angles by bending his right arm.

Try the experiment yourself.

1. **Which angle takes the least bend?**

   _____

2. **Which angle requires no bend in the arm?**

   _____

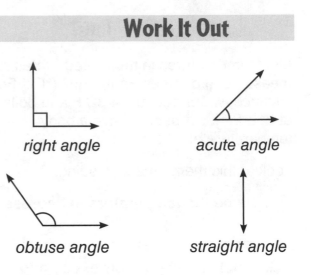

right angle   acute angle

obtuse angle   straight angle

- -

Warm-Up 154

What's the Problem?

Work It Out

Think about these different angles: right angle, acute angle, obtuse angle, and straight angle.

Which objects in your desk or the classroom can you arrange to create each of the angles?

_____

_____

_____

_____

_____

What's the Problem?

Work It Out

Lisa told Elaine that almost everything in the class seemed to have either a straight angle or a right angle. Look at these angles and see if you agree.

Find as many objects as you can that have these angles. Complete the chart.

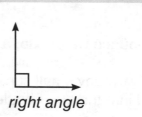

right angle   *straight angle*

Objects	Right Angle	Straight Angle

What's the Problem?

Work It Out

Elaine said that she thought just as many objects could have acute or obtuse angles.

Find as many objects as you can that have these angles. Complete the chart.

acute angle   *obtuse angle*

Objects	Acute Angle	Obtuse Angle

Measurement: liquid (ounces, cups, quarts, gallons)

Warm-Up 157

What's the Problem?

Work It Out

Noah likes to play with water. He has a 1-ounce medicine cup, an 8-ounce water cup, a quart bottle, and a gallon pail. He is constantly filling different containers to see how many small cups or medicine cups can be poured into the quart bottle or the pail.

1. **How many medicine cups will fill the 8-ounce cup?**

   _____

2. **How many 8-ounce cups will fill the quart bottle?**

   _____

3. **How many quart bottles will fill the gallon container?**

   _____

Warm-Up 158

What's the Problem?

Work It Out

Noah collected extra 1-ounce medicine cups, 8-ounce cups, and quart containers.

1. **How many 8-ounce cups can he fill with one quart jar?**

   _____

2. **How many 8-ounce cups can he fill with a gallon of water?**

   _____

3. **How many 1-ounce medicine cups can he fill with a gallon of water?**

   _____

Warm-Up 159

What's the Problem?

Work It Out

Marlene made a chart of the exact age in years and months of her friends.

Age	Friends
8 yrs./10 mos.	1
8 yrs./11 mos.	3
9 yrs./0 mos.	2
9 yrs./1 mo.	5
9 yrs./2 mos.	1
9 yrs./3 mos.	4

Age	Friends
9 yrs./4 mos.	4
9 yrs./5 mos.	0
9 yrs./6 mos.	1
9 yrs./7 mos.	0
9 yrs./8 mos.	2
9 yrs./9 mos.	1

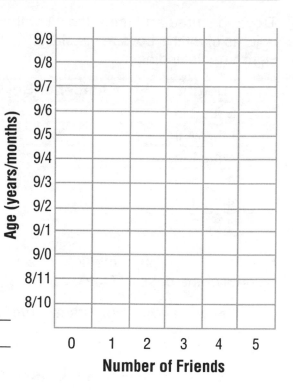

Create a bar graph on the right to illustrate the data.

1. **What information can you get from the chart about the distribution of ages?**

   _____

   _____

2. **Which are the three most common ages in the classroom?**

   _____

3. **Which are the least common ages on the chart?**

   _____

- -

Warm-Up 160

What's the Problem?

Work It Out

Take a survey to find out the ages of your classmates. Make a chart on the back of this paper to illustrate the distribution of ages in your classroom.

1. **Which are the two most common ages in your classroom?**

   _____

   _____

2. **Where are the two least common ages in your classroom?**

   _____

   _____

Warm-Up 161

What's the Problem?   ## Work It Out

Troy measured and recorded all of the
heights of all the boys in his class.
Here are his findings:

Height	Number of Boys
3 ft., 9 in.	1
3 ft., 11 in.	3
4 ft., 1 in.	3
4 ft., 3 in.	5
4 ft., 4 in.	2
4 ft., 7 in.	1

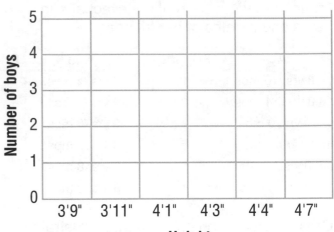

Create a bar graph to the right to show the
heights of the boys in Troy's class.

1. **Between what heights are most of the boys?**

   _____

2. **How many boys are less than 4 feet tall?**

   _____

3. **How many boys are more than 4 feet tall?**

   _____

Warm-Up 162

What's the Problem?   ## Work It Out

Make a survey of either boys or girls in your
classroom. Use a yardstick, ruler, or
measuring tape to measure their heights.
Record the heights and then make a chart or
bar graph from your findings.

**List at least 3 things you learned from the
survey and chart.**

_____

_____

_____

Warm-Up 163

What's the Problem?

Work It Out

Elaine thought about the months of the year and how many days each one has. She thought about the year 2020, which is a leap year. (It has one extra day.) Study the chart to the right to see what she discovered.

1. **How many months have 31 days?**

   _____

2. **What is the percentage of months of the year that have 30 days?**

   _____

3. **What is the average number of days per month? Express your answer as a mixed number (for example, 5 3/4).**

   _____

January	February	March
31	29	31
April	**May**	**June**
30	31	30
July	**August**	**September**
31	31	30
October	**November**	**December**
31	30	31

Warm-Up 164

What's the Problem?

Work It Out

Scott was looking at the number of days in each month in the year 2015. He made this chart to help him analyze the numbers:

1. **In which month will the 100th day of the year 2015 occur?**

   _____

2. **In which month will the 183rd day of the year 2015 occur? What is the significance of the 183rd day?**

   _____

   _____

3. **Scott's birthday is September 2nd. What day of the year (in numeral form) will that be?**

   _____

January	February	March
31	28	31
April	**May**	**June**
30	31	30
July	**August**	**September**
31	31	30
October	**November**	**December**
31	30	31

What's the Problem?   **Work It Out**

During the summer, Julian studied the 2013 and 2014 calendars to find out how many days he would have to go to school in that school year. He used several pieces of information to help him:

- School begins on September 1 and ends on June 21.

- He gets a total of 84 weekend days off and the following weekdays off for holidays:
  - 1 day for President's Day
  - 5 days for Spring Holiday
  - 1 day for Memorial Day
  - 1 day for Labor Day
  - 2 days for Thanksgiving
  - 10 days for Winter Holiday.

How many days will Julian need to go to school for the upcoming school year?

_____

What's the Problem?   **Work It Out**

Antonio looked at his upcoming school year and determined that he would be attending school on 176 weekdays.

1. **If Antonio read a book every 8 school days, how many books would he read during his school year?**

_____

2. **If Antonio missed school 1 out of every 16 days, how many days will he miss in a year?**

_____

Warm-Up 167

What's the Problem?   Work It Out

Christian wanted to find out how much time was left until school was out. It is now 9:00 A.M. exactly. School is out for the day at 2:55 P.M.

Christian knows there are 12 hours in the morning called "A.M." and 12 hours in the afternoon called "P.M." Together that makes 24 hours in one day. He also knows that there are 60 minutes in one hour and 60 seconds in one minute.

1. **How many hours are there in the morning from 9:00 A.M. to 12 noon?**

   _____

2. **How many hours and minutes are there from 12 noon to 2:55 P.M.?**

   _____

3. **What is the total time in hours and minutes?**

   _____

4. **How many total minutes did he have to wait from 9:00 A.M. to 2:55 P.M.?**

   _____

5. **How many total seconds did he have to wait?**

   _____

• •

Warm-Up 168

What's the Problem?   Work It Out

Christian's birthday party started at 6:30 P.M. and lasted until 10:15 P.M.

1. **How long did the party last in hours and minutes?**

   _____

2. **What is the total number of minutes it lasted?**

   _____

3. **How many total seconds did it last?**

   _____

Warm-Up 169

What's the Problem?   Work It Out

During the school year, Gianna usually keeps a regular sleeping schedule. She goes to bed at 9:15 P.M. and wakes up at 6:30 A.M.

1. **For how long does Gianna sleep on a school night? Express the answer in hours and minutes.**

   _____

2. **During a typical 5-day school week, about how long does Gianna sleep? Round your answer to the nearest hour.**

   _____

Warm-Up 170

What's the Problem?   Work It Out

At Clark's camp, the counselors posted the schedule for morning activities. They used military time.

1. **How long is it from the time Clark will wake up until the time he will eat lunch? Express the answer in hours and minutes.**

   _____

2. **How long will Clark's morning exercise last?**

   _____

3. **If you take away "breakfast" and "free time," for how long will Clark be engaged in activities in the morning until lunchtime?**

   _____

Time	Activity
0700	Wake up
0720	Morning exercise
0800	Breakfast
0845	Free time
0930	Classroom work
1230	Lunch

Warm-Up 171

What's the Problem?

Work It Out

Lisa took a survey of all fourth-graders in Evanwood Elementary School to determine the students' favorite sports activities. The results are shown on the survey to the right.

1. **According to Lisa's survey, which two sports were twice as popular as baseball?**

   _____

   _____

2. **How many students were surveyed altogether?**

   _____

Favorite Sport	Students
Baseball	13
Basketball	26
Volleyball	4
Football	27
Kickball	15

Warm-Up 172

What's the Problem?

Work It Out

Lisa and Armando surveyed fifth- and sixth-graders at Evanwood Elementary to find out their favorite sports. Here are the results:

1. **Which sport was exactly twice as popular as baseball?**

   _____

2. **About how many times as popular as kickball was basketball?**

   _____

3. **How many students were surveyed altogether?**

   _____

Favorite Sport	Students
Baseball	17
Basketball	51
Volleyball	13
Football	34
Kickball	3

Warm-Up 173

What's the Problem?

The fourth-graders in Ms. Ferrel's class took a survey of fast food preferences. The survey results are shown to the right.

1. **Which were the two most popular fast food places?**

   _____

   _____

2. **Which were the two least popular fast food places?**

   _____

   _____

3. **How many students are in Ms. Ferrel's class?**

   _____

Work It Out

Favorite Restaurant	Students
Simple Sam's	7
Big Mike's	8
The Nutty Burger	6
Hotdog Heaven	4
Crazy Legs	11
Freaky Fries	3

Warm-Up 174

What's the Problem?

The survey of fast food places was extended to all fourth-graders. The results are shown to the right.

1. **Which were the three most popular fast food places?**

   _____

   _____

   _____

2. **Which were the two least popular fast food places?**

   _____

   _____

3. **How many fourth-graders were surveyed?**

   _____

Work It Out

Favorite Restaurant	Students
Simple Sam's	16
Big Mike's	19
The Nutty Burger	16
Hotdog Heaven	7
Crazy Legs	29
Freaky Fries	4

What's the Problem?

Work It Out

Melissa and Eddie conducted a random sampling of 100 students in their school about their preferences for 5 cafeteria lunches. They recorded the results on the circle graph shown here:

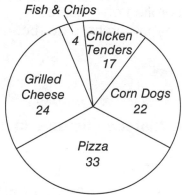

1. **What percentage of the students surveyed preferred fish and chips?**

   _____

2. **Which meal was preferred by $\frac{1}{3}$ of those asked?**

   _____

3. **Which two meals were favored by 39%?**

   _____

   _____

4. **Which meal was preferred by about $\frac{1}{4}$ of those asked?**

   _____

- -

Warm-Up 176

What's the Problem?

Work It Out

The circle graph to the right shows the lunch preferences of 100 students at Oak Ave. School. The table shows on which days certain foods are served at the school.

1. **Based on this information, on which day will the most students be likely to buy lunch?**

   _____

2. **On which day will students be most likely to bring lunch from home?**

   _____

3. **What percentage of students would be likely to buy their lunch on Thursday?**

   _____

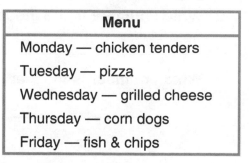

Menu
Monday — chicken tenders
Tuesday — pizza
Wednesday — grilled cheese
Thursday — corn dogs
Friday — fish & chips

Warm-Up 177

What's the Problem?   Work It Out

Max rolled one dice cube 11 times. These were the numbers he recorded:

6	2	3	6	1	1
4	2	3	6	5	

1. **List the numbers in order from least to greatest.**

   _____

2. **Which number is the mode (the most frequently occurring number)?**

   _____

3. **Which number is the median (the middle number) in this group?**

   _____

Warm-Up 178

What's the Problem?   Work It Out

Max rolled a pair of dice 9 times. He recorded the totals for each roll. They are listed here:

7	12	5	7	6
3	7	4	9	

1. **List the numbers in order from least to greatest.**

   _____

2. **Which number is the mode in this group?**

   _____

3. **Which number is the median in this group?**

   _____

Warm-Up 179

What's the Problem?

Work It Out

Mrs. Wilkins wrote the names of 5 students on 5 separate tickets and placed them in a bag for a drawing. Tommy's name was on one of the tickets.

1. **What is the probability that Tommy's name will be drawn? (Circle the letter next to the correct answer.)**

    A. 1 in 4, or 25%   C. 4 in 5, or 80%

    B. 1 in 5, or 20%   D. 5 in 5, or 100%

2. **What is the probability that *either* Jake or Robbie's name will be drawn? (Circle the letter next to the correct answer.)**

    A. 2 in 5, or 40%   C. 1 in 5, or 20%

    B. 2 in 4, or 50%   D. 5 in 5, or 100%

Tommy   Robbie

Alyssa   Jennifer

Jake

Warm-Up 180

What's the Problem?

Work It Out

Mrs. Wilkins keeps the tickets of students who don't win the daily drawing for an end-of-the-week drawing. Jennifer has 5 tickets out of 20 tickets in the end-of-the-week drawing.

1. **What is the probability that Jennifer will win the drawing? (Circle the letter next to the correct answer.)**

    A. 1 in 5, or 20%   C. 1 in 4, or 25%

    B. 15 in 20, or 75%   D. 5 in 15, or 33%

2. **What is the probability that Jennifer will not win the drawing?**

    _____

Warm-Up 181

What's the Problem?

Work It Out

Danny used an eye dropper to see how many individual drops he could get on the head of a penny before the water spilled off the penny. He did 7 trials with 7 different pennies. His results are listed to the right.

Penny	Drops
1	19
2	29
3	17
4	33
5	33
6	28
7	47

1. **Which number is the mode?**

   _____

2. **Which number is the median?**

   _____

3. **What is the range? (Subtract the smallest number from the largest number.)**

   _____

Warm-Up 182

What's the Problem?

Work It Out

Kathleen tried to see how many drops of water she could get on a penny before the water spilled. Her results are listed to the right.

Penny	Drops
1	16
2	36
3	27
4	37
5	36
6	33
7	40

1. **Which number is the mode?**

   _____

2. **Which number is the median?**

   _____

3. **What is the range?**

   _____

Warm-Up 183

What's the Problem?

Stephanie has 4 tops: a red blouse, a yellow pullover, a blue blouse, and a purple pullover. She has 4 pairs of shorts: striped, blue, brown, and black.

How many combinations of tops and shorts can she make before she has to repeat? Complete the chart to illustrate her choices.

_____

Work It Out

Tops	Shorts
red	striped
red	blue
red	

Warm-Up 184

What's the Problem?

Stephanie's school uniform can have blue, black, or khaki shorts. She can instead wear skirts in the same three colors. Her shirts may be blue, black, khaki, or maroon.

How many different combinations can she create?

_____

Make a chart to illustrate her choices.

Work It Out

Warm-Up 185

What's the Problem? **Work It Out**

Charlie flipped a penny 10 times. He recorded the heads or tails outcome for each flip.

1st	2nd	3rd	4th	5th	6th	7th	8th	9th	10th
H	H	T	H	T	H	T	T	T	H

1. **What was his fraction/percentage of heads for those 10 flips? (Circle the letter next to the correct answer.)**

   A. $\frac{5}{10} = \frac{1}{2} = 50\%$ C. $\frac{1}{4} = 25\%$

   B. $\frac{4}{10} = \frac{2}{5} = 40\%$ D. $\frac{6}{10} = \frac{3}{5} = 60\%$

- -

Warm-Up 186

What's the Problem? **Work It Out**

Let's look at Charlie's results after flipping a penny 10 times.

1st	2nd	3rd	4th	5th	6th	7th	8th	9th	10th
H	H	T	H	T	H	T	T	T	H

1. **What would be the most likely result if he flipped the penny 20 times? Explain your answer.**

   _____

   _____

2. **Why would flipping the coin 100 times or more be more likely to give $\frac{1}{2}$ or 50% as the chances of flipping heads or flipping tails?**

   _____

   _____

3. **Would it matter if the coin were a penny or a quarter?**

   _____

   _____

Warm-Up 187

What's the Problem?

Work It Out

Jack received 3 trophies—one each for baseball, football, and basketball. He wanted to arrange them on his dresser.

How many ways can he arrange the trophies on his dresser in the left, center, and right positions? Complete the chart to help you find the answer.

_____

Left	Center	Right
Baseball	Football	Basketball
Baseball	Basketball	Football
Football		

Warm-Up 188

What's the Problem?

Work It Out

Jack received a hockey trophy to go along with his baseball, football, and basketball trophies. He wanted to arrange all of his trophies on his dresser.

How many different ways can he arrange the 4 trophies?

_____

Complete the chart to help you find the answer.

1st	2nd	3rd	4th
Baseball	Football	Basketball	Hockey
Baseball			

What's the Problem?   Work It Out

Sweet Valley Elementary School encouraged students to wear college T-shirts and sweatshirts on the last Friday of each month. The tally sheet below shows the shirts worn on one Friday.

	NYU	UCLA	USC	NDU	UVA	UW	UT	UND	UNC
1st grade	/	//	///	/	/	/	/	//	/
2nd grade		///	/	/	//		//	/	//
3rd grade	//	///	//	//		/	///	/	///
4th grade	//	////	///		/	/	////		//
5th grade	///	////	/	//	///	/	/		//
6th grade	//	⫽⃥	////	/	////	//	/	/	//

1. **Which college was the favorite among first graders?**

   _____

2. **Which college was the favorite in the school?**

   _____

3. **Which college was the least favorite?**

   _____

4. **Which grade wore the most college shirts?**

   _____

• •

What's the Problem?   Work It Out

Create a survey sheet that could be used with students at your school about favorite colleges, favorite sports teams, favorite fast food places, or similar information you could use to collect data.

Your Topic: _____

Warm-Up 191

What's the Problem?

Richard rolled one die 24 times. These were the results of his rolls:

1. **Which numbers were rolled fewer than the expected times?**

   _____

2. **Which numbers were rolled more than the expected times?**

   _____

3. **Explain why 2 and 5 were rolled the number of times to be expected given the number of rolls and the number of faces on the die.**

   _____

   _____

   _____

Work It Out

1	2	3	4	5	6
X	X	X	X	X	X
X	X	X	X	X	X
X	X	X	X	X	
X	X		X	X	
X			X		
			X		

Warm-Up 192

What's the Problem?

Richard rolled a pair of dice to determine which would be the easiest and most likely totals to roll.

1. **Complete the chart to the right.**

2. **Which number is the most likely to be rolled?**

   _____

Work It Out

Number Rolled	Possible Combinations
2	1 + 1
3	1 + 2, 2 + 1
4	1 + 3, 2 + 2, 3 + 1
5	
6	
7	
8	
9	
10	
11	
12	

What's the Problem?

Work It Out

Sabrina and Marina are fourth-grade twins. Each has her name on a ticket for the Friday drawing for Student of the Week. There are 12 names in the box for the principal to draw. The twins don't care which of their names are drawn, as long as it is one of them.

1. **What is the probability that Sabrina's name will be drawn?**

   _____

2. **What is the probability that either Sabrina or Marina's name will be drawn?**

   _____

3. **What is the probability that neither name will be drawn?**

   _____

Warm-Up
194

What's the Problem?

Work It Out

Jeffrey had his name on 3 tickets in the weekly drawing, which had 12 tickets altogether.

1. **What is the probability that Jeffrey's name will be drawn? Express the answer as a fraction in two ways.**

   _____

   _____

2. **What is the probability that Jeffrey's name will not be drawn? Express the answer as a fraction in two ways.**

   _____

   _____

Data Analysis and Probability: bar graphs

What's the Problem?

Work It Out

Thomas made a bar graph to record his magazine sales
for the first week of the school fundraiser.

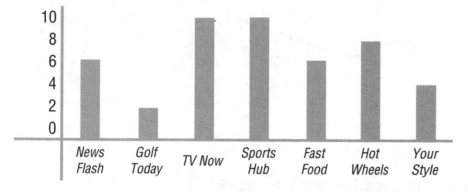

1. **Which were Thomas' two best-selling magazines?**

   _____

2. **Which were his two weakest-selling magazines?**

   _____

• •

What's the Problem?

Work It Out

Thomas had the following sales for the
second week of the fundraiser.

Magazine	Sold
News Flash	12 subscriptions
Golf Today	3 subscriptions
TV Now	5 subscriptions
Sports Hub	9 subscriptions
Fast Food	7 subscriptions
Hot Wheels	15 subscriptions
Your Style	10 subscriptions

Make a bar graph to illustrate his sales.

Warm-Up 197

What's the Problem?   Work It Out

Alexandra created a **line** graph to show how many minutes she read every evening for a week.

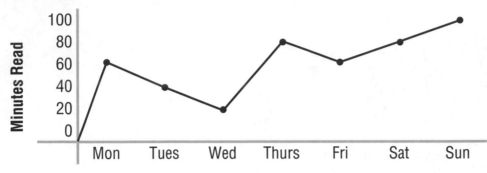

1. **How many minutes did Alexandra read during the week?**

   _____

2. **Which nights did she read the most?**

   _____

3. **Which two nights did she read at least twice as much as Tuesday night?**

   _____

Warm-Up 198

What's the Problem?   Work It Out

Alexandra read the following minutes during the second week: Monday, 30; Tuesday, 40; Wednesday, 20; Thursday, 50; Friday, 10; Saturday, 80; Sunday, 100.

Create a line graph below to record Alexandra's minutes.

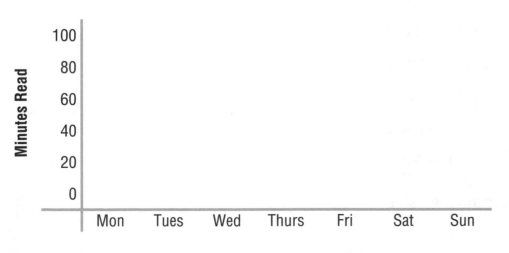

Warm-Up 199

What's the Problem?   Work It Out

This graph shows the hours Lori spent practicing soccer in one week.

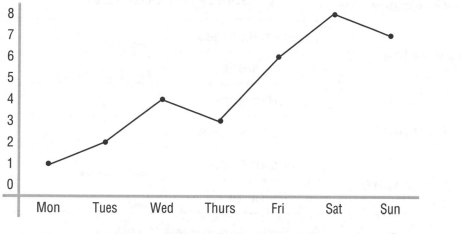

1. **How many hours did Lori practice soccer on Tuesday?** _____

2. **Which two days did she spend the least time on soccer?**

   _____

3. **How many hours of the week did she spend on soccer altogether?** _____

Warm-Up 200

What's the Problem?   Work It Out

Jeremiah is very involved in making a fleet of model ships over a 6-week period. During the 1st week, he spent 8 hours. Then he spent 16 hours during the 2nd week, 12 hours during the 3rd week, 22 hours during the 4th week, and 24 hours during 5th week. He finished the project in the 6th week, when he spent a total of 26 hours.

Use the frame to the right to create a line graph showing Jeremiah's time spent on model ships in the 6-week period.

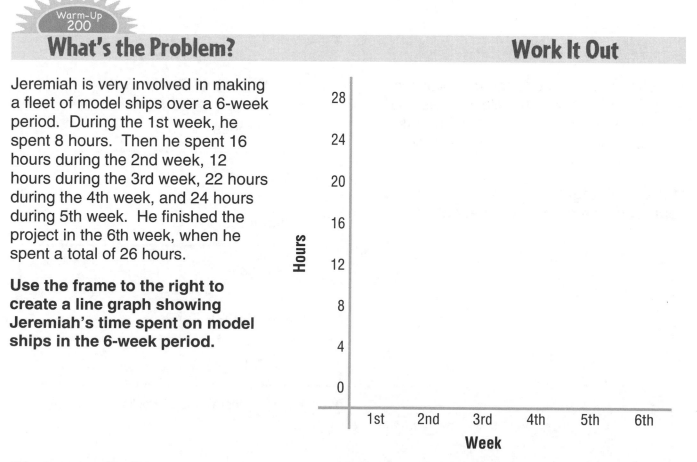

Data Analysis and Probability: pictographs

What's the Problem?

Work It Out

Lorena made a pictograph to illustrate types of books read by her classmates in October. Study the graph to the right.

1. **Which category of books was the most popular?**

   _____

2. **Which books were the least popular?**

   _____

3. **How many more sports stories were read than adventures?**

   _____

4. **How many books were read altogether?**

   _____

Survey of Books Read

animal stories	▯ ▯ ▯
mysteries	▯ ▯ ▯ ▯
adventures	▯ ▯
sports stories	▯ ▯ ▯ ▯ ▯
humor (funny)	▯ ▯ ▯
other	▯

Key: Each ▯ represents 10 books.

- -

What's the Problem?

Work It Out

In November, Lori collected the following information on books her classmates read: 40 mysteries, 50 funny books, 20 sports books, 60 adventures, 20 animal stories, and 20 other books.

Use the pictograph frame to the right to represent the data she collected.

Survey of Books Read

animal stories	
mysteries	
adventures	
sports	
humor (funny)	
other	

Key: Each ▯ represents 10 books.

Data Analysis and Probability: bar graphs

What's the Problem?

Work It Out

Danny made this bar graph showing how he used his time on an average school day.

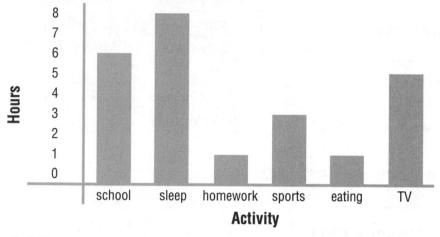

1. **What does Danny spend most of his time doing?**

   _____

2. **What does he spend most of his time doing when he is not in school or asleep?**

   _____

3. **What does he spend 5 times as much time doing as homework?**

   _____

What's the Problem?

Work It Out

Nicholas spends an average day in the summer time doing the following activities: sleeping, 9 hours; eating, 2 hours; exercise, 1 hour; watching TV, 4 hours; playing video games, 5 hours; playing drums, 2 hours; doing chores, 1 hour.

On the back of this paper, make a bar graph to illustrate his day.

Warm-Up 205

What's the Problem?

Work It Out

Dominic and Diana checked the cereal choices of fourth-graders and recorded the results on the tally sheet to the right.

1. **Which was the most popular cereal?**

   _____

2. **Which cereal was least popular?**

   _____

3. **How many fourth-graders were surveyed?**

   _____

4. **Which 2 cereals together were chosen 30 times?**

   _____ _____

5. **Which 3 cereals together were chosen the same number of times as another cereal?**

   _____ _____

   _____

Cereal Name	# of Students
Crispy Corns	卌 卌 //
Special Q	卌 //
Oaty Oats	卌 卌 卌 ///
Corny Bits	///
Wheat Flakes	卌 卌 /
Rice Soggies	//

Warm-Up 206

What's the Problem?

Work It Out

Doug decided to check the cereal choices of second-graders and recorded the results on the tally sheet to the right.

1. **Which was the most popular cereal?**

   _____

2. **Which cereal was least popular?**

   _____

3. **How many second-graders were surveyed?**

   _____

4. **Which cereal was chosen exactly half as often as another?**

   _____

Cereal Name	# of Students
Crispy Corns	卌 /
Special Q	卌 //
Oaty Oats	卌 卌 卌 卌 卌 /
Corny Bits	卌 卌 ///
Wheat Flakes	卌 /
Rice Soggies	///

Warm-Up 207

What's the Problem?

Work It Out

There is a daily drawing where one child gets to draw a marble out of a bag. Two of the marbles are plain black marbles. Two of the marbles are bluish-green shiners, and one marble is a very valuable Ultra Special Golden Cat's Eye.

Henry has been chosen this week to draw a marble.

1. **What are the chances that Henry will draw a black marble?**

   _____

2. **What are the chances that he will draw a bluish-green shiner?**

   _____

3. **What is the probability that Henry will draw the Ultra Special Golden Cat's Eye?**

   _____

4. **What is the probability that he will not draw the Ultra Special Golden Cat's Eye?**

   _____

Warm-Up 208

What's the Problem?

Work It Out

There are 8 marbles in this drawing. Two are black marbles, and two are white marbles. Two are the Red Eye Marvels, one is a blue-green shiner, and one is the very valuable Golden Cat's Eye.

1. **What are the chances that you will draw either a black or white marble?**

   _____

2. **What are the chances that you will draw a bluish-green shiner?**

   _____

3. **What is the probability that you will draw either a black, white, or red marble?**

   _____

4. **What is the probability that you will draw the Golden Cat's Eye?**

   _____

Warm-Up 209

What's the Problem?

Mario conducted a survey of his classmates to determine their favorite pizza topping:

1. **How many of his classmates preferred pepperoni?**

   _____

2. **How many students did Mario survey?**

   _____

3. **How many preferred either pepperoni or bacon?**

   _____

4. **Which were the two least popular toppings?**

   _____

   _____

5. **What percentage of students preferred double cheese?**

   _____

Work It Out

Favorite Pizza Toppings

Double Cheese	⊬⊬ //
Pepperoni	⊬⊬ ⊬⊬
Sausage	///
Pineapple	////
Bacon	⊬⊬ /
Broccoli	/
Other	////

· ·

Warm-Up 210

What's the Problem?

Create your own survey and tally list in the space below. Choose one of the topics listed or create a topic of your choice that will bring a variety of responses from your classmates. List possible choices. Add others suggested by classmates or add an "Other" category.

Share your results with a classmate.

Work It Out

Survey Choices

Favorite Pizza Toppings

Favorite Ice Cream Flavor

Favorite Music Group

Favorite Television Show

Favorite Sports Team

Favorite Color

Warm-Up 211

What's the Problem?

Work It Out

Adrian doesn't know how many marbles he has in a bag. He does know that if he takes 12 marbles away from the bag of marbles he will have 30 marbles. He writes the equation this way:

$$n - 12 = 30$$

How many marbles are in the bag (n)?

_____

Warm-Up 212

What's the Problem?

Work It Out

Adrian's sister took 15 marbles out of a bag and then gave the rest to her brother. The bag her brother received had 35 marbles in it.

How many marbles were in the bag to begin with? Solve this equation:
$n - 15 = 35$.

_____

Algebra: algebraic symbols

Warm-Up 213

What's the Problem?

Jose created a dictionary of symbols used in algebra.

Use Jose's dictionary to compute the answer to this inequality:

$(9)(4) > \dfrac{20}{4}$

_____ is greater than _____

Work It Out

= is "equal to"

≠ is "not equal to"

> is "greater than"

< is "less than"

( ) and • both mean "multiply by"

— is "divided by"

Warm-Up 214

What's the Problem?

Jose created a dictionary of symbols used in algebra.

Use Jose's dictionary to compute the answers to these math sentences:

1. $\dfrac{24}{4} > (3)(1)$ _____

2. $6 • 5 = 10(3)$ _____

3. $7(4) > 3(7)$ _____

Work It Out

= is "equal to"

≠ is "not equal to"

> is "greater than"

< is "less than"

( ) and • both mean "multiply by"

— is "divided by"

Warm-Up 215

What's the Problem?

Work It Out

David has 16 skate wheels, which he is putting on 4 boards to go with the 3 boards he has.

How many boards does he have altogether? Simplify the expression.

$$\frac{16}{4} + 3 =$$

_____

Warm-Up 216

What's the Problem?

Work It Out

Michelle needs to evaluate this expression in order to determine how many gumballs should go into each package:

$$\frac{100}{n} + 6, \text{ where } n \text{ equals } 10$$

_____

Warm-Up 217

What's the Problem?

Work It Out

Monique needs to know what number times 15 equals 45.

Solve this equation.

t x 15 = 45

_____

Warm-Up 218

What's the Problem?

Work It Out

Monique is packing 20 chocolates into each box. She has 80 chocolate candies.

1. **How many boxes does she need? Solve the equation.**

$$\frac{80}{n} = 20$$

_____

2. **How many boxes does she need if she packs only 10 chocolates into each box? Solve the equation.**

$$\frac{80}{n} = 10$$

_____

**Warm-Up
219**

What's the Problem?

Work It Out

Edwin knew that an expression with an exponent means the base is multiplied by itself. Therefore, 3^2 (or, "3 to the second power") means to multiply 3 x 3, which equals 9. He needs to fill a box of large marbles with 7 rows holding 7 marbles each. This is written as "7^2."

How many marbles does Edwin need?

_____

**Warm-Up
220**

What's the Problem?

Work It Out

Edwin wanted to know what number to the second power would equal 144.

What number times itself equals 144?

_____

Warm-Up 221

What's the Problem?

Work It Out

Davis is looking for a pattern between fiction and nonfiction as he straightens the books returned to the library. Study the chart to the right.

1. **What are the missing numbers? Fill in the chart.**

2. **What is the pattern for the function?**

_____

_____

_____

	Fiction	Nonfiction
Monday	20	10
Tuesday	30	15
Wednesday	18	
Thursday	14	
Friday		11

- -

Warm-Up 222

What's the Problem?

Work It Out

Davis found a pattern in the books returned to the library by third- and fourth-graders. He began to make the chart on the right to record his findings.

1. **What are the missing numbers? Fill in the chart.**

2. **What is the pattern for this function?**

_____

_____

_____

	Third Grade	Fourth Grade
Week 1	60	67
Week 2	77	84
Week 3		56
Week 4	76	
Week 5		70

What's the Problem?

Work It Out

When the math blocks were returned, Adriana discovered that 5 of the 12 blocks were missing in one box, and 3 of the 12 blocks were missing in another box. She wrote it as an equation:

$$(12 - 5) + (12 - 3) = n$$

Solve the equation. (Remember to do the work in the parentheses first).

_____

What's the Problem?

Work It Out

Adriana was in charge of making sure all of the math blocks were turned in after playtime. She wrote these equations to show how many blocks were missing (n) from the two boxes turned in:

Box 1: $(12 - n) = 7$

Box 2: $(12 - n) = 3$

1. **Solve the equations to find out how many blocks were missing in each box.**

_____

_____

2. **Write two more equations using parentheses and *n*.**

_____

_____

Warm-Up 225

What's the Problem?

Work It Out

During a marbles game, Claudia won 9 marbles but lost 6. Then she won 12 more marbles but lost 4.

She wrote this equation to illustrate the problem:

$9 - 6 + 12 - 4 = n$

Solve the equation. How many marbles did Claudia win?

_____

Warm-Up 226

What's the Problem?

Work It Out

In a game, Claudia won 14 marbles and lost 5. Then she won 20 marbles and lost 6. Finally she won 7 more marbles.

1. **Write an equation to show Claudia's wins and losses.**

   _____

2. **Solve the equation to show how many marbles she won during the game.**

   _____

Warm-Up 227

What's the Problem?

Work It Out

Tori was playing a party game with cards and beads. She started with 3 beads and drew a red 10, which allowed her to multiply 10 times the 3. Then she drew a black 2, which required her to divide her number of beads by 2. Then she drew a red 6, which allowed her to multiply her beads by 6.

Tori wrote this equation to express how many beads she won:

$$3 \times 10 \div 2 \times 6 = n$$

Solve the equation.

_____

Warm-Up 228

What's the Problem?

Work It Out

During a game, Tori started out with 5 beads and drew a card from the deck. It was a red 9, which allowed her to multiply her number of beads times 9. She then drew a black 3, which required her to divide her beads by 3. Then she drew a red ace, which allowed her to multiply her beads by 20.

1. **Write the equation for Tori's bead total.**

   _____

2. **Solve the equation. How many beads does Tori now have?**

   _____

Warm-Up 229

What's the Problem?

Work It Out

Carl played a card game with a friend. He started with 10 points and then got to multiply his points by 3. He then had to divide his points by 5. He then added 7 more points but lost 4 points.

He wrote this equation to express his points:

$$10 \times 3 \div 5 + 7 - 4 = n$$

Solve the equation.

_____

Warm-Up 230

What's the Problem?

Work It Out

Carl started a card game with 25 points. He then drew a 10, which he was allowed to multiply by 3 and then divide by 6.

This is Carl's equation:

$$25 + ((10 \times 3) \div 6) = n$$

Solve Carl's equation.

_____

Warm-Up 231

What's the Problem?

Work It Out

Albert has a very eccentric uncle. He likes to give money away . . . if you can solve his math problems using algebra. He offered Albert the total of $20 plus $10 minus $5—all times itself.

Albert wrote the equation this way:

$(20 + 10 - 5)^2 = n$

Solve his equation. How much money did his uncle give Albert?

_____

Warm-Up 232

What's the Problem?

Work It Out

Albert's uncle made him another offer: he would pay him the total of $20 minus $10 plus $5—all times itself, if Albert could use algebra to solve the problem.

Albert wrote the equation this way:

$(20 - 10 + 5)^2 = n$

Solve his equation. How much money did his uncle give Albert?

_____

Warm-Up 233

What's the Problem?   Work It Out

Lauren's mom offered her 11 charms to add to her bracelet. Lauren wanted a different charm for every day of the month. She wanted 30 charms. This is the equation she wrote to express how many more charms she needed.

$$n + 11 = 30$$

Solve the equation for Lauren.

_____

· ·

Warm-Up 234

What's the Problem?   Work It Out

Lauren collected a total of 17 charms. She decided she wanted a total of 31 charms so that she had a different charm to wear even in long months.

1. **Write an equation to show how many charms she needs.**

   _____

2. **Solve the equation.**

   _____

Warm-Up 235

What's the Problem?

Work It Out

James wrote an expression to indicate how much water he would use in a chemical formula.

$w + 20 - 6$, where $w = 23$

Evaluate his expression.

_____

Warm-Up 236

What's the Problem?

Work It Out

In his second expression, James indicated how many milliliters of water (w) and how many milliliters of vinegar (v) he would use in a different chemical formula.

$2w + 4v - 5$, where $w = 10$ and $v = 5$

Evaluate his expression.

_____

Warm-Up 237

What's the Problem?

Work It Out

Michelle plans to become a research chemist. She is working on formulas for a special kind of lotion. She wrote her formula with this expression.

$3(w) + p - 6$ for $w = 12$ and $p = 5$

Evaluate Michelle's expression.

_____

Warm-Up 238

What's the Problem?

Work It Out

Michelle created a more complicated formula written with this expression.

$7(w) - 12 + 4(p) - 7$ for $w = 10$ and $p = 4$

Evaluate Michelle's expression.

_____

Warm-Up 239

What's the Problem?

Work It Out

Mario wrote this inequality to express the number of milliliters of salt water in a solution:

$$12 + s < 15$$

1. **Which three whole numbers would be the only possible correct answers? (Circle the letter next to the correct answer.)**

   A. 2, 3, 4   **C. 0, 1, 2**

   B. 1, 2, 3   **D. 3, 4, 5**

2. **Explain your answer in terms of the < sign.**

   _____

   _____

Warm-Up 240

What's the Problem?

Work It Out

Mario wrote this inequality to express the number of milliliters of petroleum in a solution:

$$9 + p > 12$$

1. **Which three whole numbers would be the only possible correct answers of the ones given? (Circle the letter next to the correct answer.)**

   A. 2, 3, 4   **C. 3, 4, 5**

   B. 0, 1, 2   **D. 4, 5, 6**

2. **Explain your answer in terms of the > sign.**

   _____

   _____

Warm-Up 241

What's the Problem?   Work It Out

Cynthia wrote this algebraic expression on the board: $r + t - 5 > 0$.

1. **Which values for *r* and *t* would make this expression true? (Circle the letter next to the correct answer.)**

   A. **r = 2 and t = 3**

   B. **r = 3 and t = 2**

   C. **r = 4 and t = 2**

   D. **r = 2 and t = 1**

2. **Explain your answer in terms of the > sign.**

   _____

   _____

- -

Warm-Up 242

What's the Problem?   Work It Out

Cynthia wrote the following expression:
$p + t - 6 \neq 22$.

1. **Which of the following is the only incorrect value? (Circle the letter next to the correct answer.)**

   A. **p = 12 and t = 11**

   B. **p = 10 and t = 17**

   C. **p = 20 and t = 8**

   D. **p = 13 and t = 12**

2. **Explain your answer in terms of the ≠ sign.**

   _____

   _____

Algebra: missing factors

What's the Problem?

Work It Out

Angel is expected to bring $121 to the office for a school magazine fundraiser. Each magazine subscription cost $11. How many subscriptions does he need to sell?

He wrote the equation this way:

$11 \times s = 121$

Solve the equation.

_____

What's the Problem?

Work It Out

Angel hopes to collect $3 from as many relatives and neighbors as he can for the school jogathon held to raise money for playground equipment. He wants to raise $60.

1. **Write the equation that shows how many relatives and neighbors Angel needs to help him meet his goal.**

   _____

2. **Solve the equation you wrote above. How many relatives and neighbors does Angel need to help?**

   _____

Warm-Up 245

What's the Problem?

Work It Out

Eddie sold Christmas cards to make some money during the holiday season. He sold 5 boxes at $20 per box to one customer. He gave a discount to the customer of $16 for buying so many cards.

He wrote the equation this way to show how much money the customer owed:

$$5 (20) - 16 = n$$

1. **Solve the equation.**

   _____

2. **How much money did the customer owe?**

   _____

Warm-Up 246

What's the Problem?

Work It Out

Eddie sold 9 boxes of cards to Mrs. Jones at $8 a box. Mrs. Jones got a discount of $13 for ordering this many cards.

1. **Write an equation to show the cost and discount.**

   _____

2. **Solve the equation. How much money did Mrs. Jones owe?**

   _____

What's the Problem?

Work It Out

Allison made $11 for doing her chores. She had to pay $3 in fines at the library and $5 for talking too long on the phone. She had $7 in her savings bank. She wrote a number sentence to see how much money she still has.

Number sentence: $7 + 11 - 3 - 5 = x$

1. Complete the number sentence.

_____

2. How much money does she have?

_____

• •

Warm-Up 248

What's the Problem?

Work It Out

Allison started the week with $18, and she made $7 dollars for babysitting and $6 for doing her chores. She was charged $6 for talking too long on the phone and $3 for forgetting to make her bed every day.

Write a number sentence to determine how much money Allison now has.

_____

Warm-Up 249

What's the Problem?

Work It Out

Joshua created the sequence of numbers below to illustrate how fast his colony of snails was growing in his snail terrarium. He noticed a pattern forming.

2, 5, 9, 14, 20, ____, ____, ____, ____, ____

1. **Complete his sequence.**

2. **Describe the pattern used in his sequence.**

_____

_____

_____

Warm-Up 250

What's the Problem?

Work It Out

Joshua used this sequence of numbers to describe the growth of his cricket colony, which he keeps in a special habitat. He noticed a pattern forming.

2, 5, 11, 23, ____, ____, ____, ____, ____

1. **Complete his sequence.**

2. **Describe the pattern used in his sequence.**

_____

_____

_____

Warm-Up 1

8 teams play 4 games; 4 teams play 2 games; 2 teams play 1 game

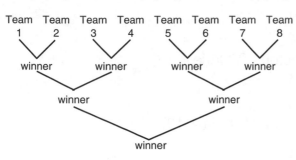

Total games: 7

Warm-Up 2

Elena — first place

↓

Chris — second place

↓

Allie — third place

↓

Derrick — fourth place

↓

Bart — fifth place

↓

Elena beat. Chris	Chris beat. Allie	Allie beat. Derrick	Derrick beat. Bart
→	→	→	→

Warm-Up 3

1st—Yankees

2nd—Red Sox

3rd —Angels

4th—Giants

Giants = 9 wins

Angels = 9 + 5 = 14 wins

Red Sox = 14 + 3 = 17 wins

Yankees = 17 + 2 = 19 wins

Warm-Up 4

Jimmy — faster than Estevan

↓

Estevan — faster than Randy

↓

Randy — faster than Sergio

↓

Sergio

Warm-Up 5

Amy = 19 + 13 = 32 shells

↓

Allison = 19 shells

↓

Anmol = 19 − 6 = 13 shells

↓

Alicia = 13 − 4 = 9 shells

Total = 32 + 19 + 13 + 9 = 73 shells

Warm-Up 6

Nathan = 24 + 3 = 27

Joshua = 18 + 6 = 24

James = 11 + 7 = 18

Albert = 11 pails

Justin = 11 − 1 = 10

Total = 27 + 24 + 18 + 11 + 10 = 90 pails

Warm-Up 7

Equilateral triangle:

Parallelogram:

Hexagon:

Warm-Up 8

Valerie = least hearts

↓

Victoria (Valerie + 12)

↓

Violet (Victoria + 13)

↓

Vicki (Violet + 7) = most hearts

Warm-Up 9

4 portions:

8 portions:

Warm-Up 10

Jason = 19 bags

Joshua = Jason + 15 = 34 bags

Arlene = Joshua + 1 bag = 35 bags

Brandon = Arlene + 9 = 44 bags

April = Brandon − 3 bags = 41 bags

Keith = Joshua − 5 bags = 29 bags

Warm-Up 11

Day	# of Nickels
Sunday	1
Monday	3
Tuesday	9
Wednesday	27
Thursday	81
Friday	243

Warm-Up 12

Bought Tickets	Free Tickets
7	3
14	6
21	9
28	12
35	15
42	18
49	21
56	24

Total Tickets: 56 + 24 = 80

ANSWER KEY (cont.)

Warm-Up 13

Day	# of Laps
1st day	2 laps
2nd day	3 laps
3rd day	5 laps
4th day	8 laps
5th day	12 laps
6th day	17 laps
7th day	23 laps
8th day	30 laps
9th day	38 laps
10th day	47 laps

Pattern adds 1 more lap than added the previous day (i.e., 1 lap after Day 1, 2 laps after Day 2, etc.).

Warm-Up 14

Day	# of Minutes
1st day	1 minute
2nd day	3 minutes
3rd day	7 minutes
4th day	15 minutes
5th day	31 minutes
6th day	63 minutes

The amount of time added doubles each day (i.e., 2 minutes added after Day 1, 4 minutes added after Day 2, etc.).

Warm-Up 15

Car	Empty Seats	Occupied Seats
1st car	5	3
2nd car	5	3
3rd car	5	3
4th car	5	3
5th car	5	3
6th car	5	3
7th car	5	3
8th car	5	3
9th car	5	3
10th car	5	3
11th car	5	3
12th car	5	3
Total	60	36

Warm-Up 16

Perfect Apples	Picked Apples
5	9
10	18
15	27
20	36
25	45
30	54
35	63
40	72
45	81
50	90
55	99
60	108

Of 108 apples picked, 60 were perfect.

Warm-Up 17

Fiction	Adventure
10	7
20	14
30	21
40	28
50	35
60	42
70	49
80	56
90	63
100	70
110	77
120	84
130	91
140	98

There were a total of 98 adventure books.

Warm-Up 18

Total Gliders	Airborne for 1 Min.	Not Airborne for 1 Min.
7	5	2
14	10	4
21	15	6
28	20	8
35	25	10
42	30	12

Elizabeth has 30 gliders that stay airborne for more than 1 minute.

Warm-Up 19

Children	Sundaes	Cake	Candy
10	5	3	2
20	10	6	4
30	15	9	6
40	20	12	8

With 40 students, 20 would prefer sundaes, 12 would prefer cake, and 8 would prefer candy.

Warm-Up 20

	Blouse	Shorts
1.	red	white
2.	red	black
3.	blue	white
4.	blue	black
5.	yellow	white
6.	yellow	black

She can wear 6 different combinations.

Warm-Up 21

Trip 1: Farmer takes chicken across the river.

Trip 2: Farmer comes back.

Trip 3: Farmer takes dog across the river, puts chicken in the boat.

Trip 4: Farmer comes back, drops off chicken, and puts corn in the boat.

Trip 5: Farmer takes corn across the river and drops it off on other side.

Trip 6: Farmer comes back and picks up chicken.

Trip 7: Farmer crosses the river with the chicken.

Farmer will need to make 7 trips across the river.

Warm-Up 22

Step one: silver dollar → penny

Step two: penny → quarter → dime

Step three: → half dollar

Final order: silver dollar → penny → quarter → dime → half dollar

Warm-Up 23

blue card = 10 points

black card = 5 points (1/2 of blue)

red card = 20 points (twice blue)

3 black cards = 15 points

3 blue cards = 30 points

3 red cards = 60 points

Total = 105 points

Warm-Up 24

Jill = 75 yards from shore

	Swim	Rest	Distance From Shore
			75 yards
1.	– 20	+ 5	60 yards
2.	– 20	+ 5	45 yards
3.	– 20	+ 5	30 yards
4.	– 20	+ 5	15 yards
5.	– 20	+ 5	0 yards

Jill swam and rested 5 times.

Warm-Up 25

Student 1 shakes with — Student 2 / Student 3 / Student 4

Student 2 shakes with — Student 3 / Student 4

Student 3 shakes with — Student 4

Total number of handshakes: 6

Warm-Up 26

Carrie tossed beanbag with — Bobby / Irene / Joey

Bobby tossed beanbag with — Irene / Joey

Irene tossed beanbag with — Joey

Total number of tosses: 6

Warm-Up 27

Use other students or objects to represent the 5 snails.

Racing Order:

1st: Muddy Max

2nd: Fearless Freddy

3nd: Dashing Dan

4th: Slippery Sam

5th: Happy Harry

Warm-Up 28

Weigh any 3 marbles on one side of the scale and any 3 on the other side of the scale.

If the 2 sides are equal . . .
1. Take the six marbles you have just weighed and set them aside.
2. Next, weigh one of the remaining marbles on each side of the scale.
   - If one marble is heavier, it is the valuable one.
   - If both marbles are the same, the remaining marble is the heavier one.

If the 2 sides are *not* equal . . .
1. Weigh two of the 3 marbles from the heavier side.
   - If one is heavier, it is the valuable marble.
   - If the marbles are equal in weight, the remaining marble is the heavier marble.

Warm-Up 29

Shape 1
3 ft. / 3 ft. / 3 ft. / 3 ft.

Shape 2
4 ft. / 4 ft. / 4 ft.

Shape 3
3 ft. / 3 ft. / 3 ft. / 3 ft.

Shape 4
2 ft. / 2 ft. / 2 ft. / 2 ft. / 2 ft. / 2 ft.

Shape 5
1 ft. / 1 ft. / 1 ft. / 1 ft. / 1 ft. / 1 ft. / 1 ft. / 1 ft.

Warm-Up 30

Jamie = 80 pages

Jennifer = 40 pages

Third reader = 20 pages

Fourth reader = 10 pages

Fifth reader = 5 pages

Total pages = 155 pages

ANSWER KEY (cont.)

Warm-Up 31

Know:
- perimeter = 300 feet
- length = 10 feet longer than width

Guesses:

Length	Width	Perimeter
20 ft.	10 ft.	60 ft.
40 ft.	30 ft.	140 ft.
60 ft.	50 ft.	220 ft.
70 ft.	60 ft.	260 ft.
75 ft.	65 ft.	280 ft.
80 ft.	70 ft.	300 ft.

Answer: The pool is 80 ft. long and 70 ft. wide.

Warm-Up 32

Know:
- ice cream cone cost $3.50
- used 7 more dimes than quarters

Guesses:

Quarters	Dimes	Total Money
1— $0.25	8 — $0.80	$1.05
4 — $1.00	11 — $1.10	$2.10
6 — $1.50	13 — $1.30	$2.80
8 — $2.00	15 — $1.50	$3.50

Answer: She used 8 quarters and 15 dimes.

Warm-Up 33

Know:
- 28 total balls
- 3 more softballs than kickballs
- 2 fewer footballs than kickballs
- 4 more volleyballs than softballs

	Guess 1	Guess 2	Guess 3	Guess 4
volleyballs (+4)	9	10	11	12
softballs (+3)	5	6	7	8
kickballs	2	3	4	5
footballs (−2)	0	1	2	3
Total	16	20	24	28

Warm-Up 34

Know:
- Derrick's dad is 30.
- Derrick is 8.

	Derrick	Dad
Guess 1:	10	32
Guess 2:	12	34
Guess 3:	14	36
Guess 4:	16	38
Guess 5:	18	40
Guess 6:	20	42
Guess 7:	21	43
Guess 8:	22	44

Answer: Derrick will be 22 when his father is 44.

Warm-Up 35

Know:
- Children's tickets cost $5.
- Adult's tickets cost $8.
- $72 were spent on tickets.

	$5 Children's	$8 Adult's	Total
Guess 1:	2 — $10	6 — $48	$58
Guess 2:	3 — $15	8 — $64	$79
Guess 3:	4 — $20	4 — $32	$52
Guess 4:	6 — $30	4 — $32	$62
Guess 5:	8 — $40	4 — $32	$72

Answer: Her father bought 8 children's tickets and 4 adult tickets.

Warm-Up 36

Know:
- Each letter must stand for a single-digit number. Possible answers include:

Problem #1	Problem #2	Problem #3	Problem #4	Problem #5
111 + 222 333	222 + 333 555	333 + 444 777	444 + 555 999	555 + 222 777

Problem #6	Problem #7	Problem #8	Problem #9	Problem #10
111 + 333 444	222 + 444 666	333 + 555 888	111 + 444 555	222 + 777 999

Warm-Up 37

Know: Need to make $0.50.

Combination 1: 2 quarters

Combination 2: 5 dimes

Combination 3: 10 nickels

Combination 4: 1 dime, 3 nickels, 1 quarter

Combination 5: 2 dimes, 1 nickel, 1 quarter

Combination 6: 3 dimes, 4 nickels

Combination 7: 4 dimes, 2 nickels

Combination 8: 1 dime, 8 nickels

Combination 9: 2 dimes, 6 nickels

Combination 10: 1 quarter, 5 nickels

Warm-Up 38

Know:

- paid $2.65
- 11 more nickels than quarters

Quarters	Nickels	Total ($2.65)
1	12	$0.85
3	14	$1.45
5	16	$2.05
6	17	$2.35
7	18	$2.65

Answer: Tiffany used 7 quarters and 18 nickels to pay for the mouse.

Warm-Up 39

Know:

- Sharon picked 65 apples in 5 days.
- Each day, she picked 4 more apples than the day before.

	Day 1	Day 2	Day 3	Day 4	Day 5	Total
Guess 1:	1	5	9	13	17	45
Guess 2:	2	6	10	14	18	50
Guess 3:	3	7	11	15	19	55
Guess 4:	4	8	12	16	20	60
Guess 5:	5	9	13	17	21	65

Answer: She picked 5 on Day 1, 9 on Day 2, 13 on Day 3, 17 on Day 4, and 21 on Day 5.

Warm-Up 40

Know:

- Sherrie is 9.
- Sherrie's mom is 29.

	Sherrie	Her Mom
Guess 1:	9	29
Guess 2:	12	32
Guess 3:	15	35
Guess 4:	17	37
Guess 5:	19	39
Guess 6:	20	40

Answer: Sherrie will be 20 when her mom is 40.

Warm-Up 41

Month	Books Read
September	3
October	6
November	9
December	12
January	15
February	18

Pattern: She reads 3 more books every month than she did the previous month.

Answer: She will read 18 books in February.

Warm-Up 42

Month	Cards
February	3
March	5
April	8
May	12
June	17
July	23
August	30
September	38
October	47

Total: 183

Pattern: He collects 1 more each month than he collected the previous month.

Answer: He will have collected a total of 183 cards by October 31.

Warm-Up 43

Week	Miles
1	1
2	2
3	4
4	8
5	16
6	32

Pattern: She rides twice as many miles per day as she did the previous week.

Answer: She rode 32 miles on the 6th week.

Warm-Up 44

Month	Friends
January	2
February	8
March	32
April	128
May	512
June	2,048

Pattern: She meets 4 times as many friends each month as she did the previous month.

Answer: She will meet 2,048 friends in June.

Warm-Up 45

Day	Stickers	Total Stickers
1	6	6
2	9	15
3	12	27
4	15	42
5	18	60
6	21	81
7	24	105
8	27	132

Answer: Sharon had 132 stickers after 8 days.

Warm-Up 46

Week	Pennies
1st	1
2nd	2
3rd	4
4th	8
5th	16
6th	32
7th	64
8th	128
9th	256
10th	512
11th	1,024

Pattern: He added twice as many pennies each week as were added the previous week.

Answer: He added more than 1,000 pennies on the 11th week.

Warm-Up 47

Week	Songs
1st	3
2nd	4
3rd	6
4th	9
5th	13
6th	18
7th	24
8th	31

Pattern: Add one extra song learned each week.

Answer: After 8 weeks, she knew 31 songs.

Warm-Up 48

Day	Given	Left
1st	48	48
2nd	24	24
3rd	12	12
4th	6	6
5th	3	3

Pattern: He gave away half of his remaining candies each day.

Answer: Harvey will have 3 candies left on the fifth day.

Warm-Up 49

Ring	People Entering	Total People at Party
1st	1	2
2nd	3	5
3rd	5	10
4th	7	17
5th	9	26
6th	11	37
7th	13	50
8th	15	65
9th	17	82
10th	19	101

Pattern: Add 2 more people on each ring.

Answers: 19 people will enter on the 10th ring, and then there will be 101 people at the party.

Warm-Up 50

Pattern: Add a number each time the number goes up (one 1, two 2s, three 3s, etc.)

Answer: 1, 2, 2, 3, 3, 3, 4, **4, 4, 4, 5, 5, 5, 5, 5, 6**

Warm-Up 51
$5,400

Warm-Up 52
$454.14

Warm-Up 53
1. $10.49
2. $2.54

Warm-Up 54
1. No, she only has $17.71.
2. She needs $0.27 more.

Warm-Up 55
$7.05

Warm-Up 56
$53.00

Warm-Up 57
8 dozen (or 96) fruits and vegetables

Warm-Up 58
14 dozen (or 168) fruits and vegetables

Warm-Up 59
12 pages

Warm-Up 60
38 pages

Warm-Up 61
100 points

Warm-Up 62
13 points

Warm-Up 63
5/8

Warm-Up 64
5/6

Warm-Up 65
Rudy and Elaine

Warm-Up 66
1. Patrick
2. 1/8 more

Warm-Up 67
C

Warm-Up 68
C

Warm-Up 69
D

Warm-Up 70
B

Warm-Up 71
75/100 or ¾

Warm-Up 72
60/100 = 6/10 = 3/5

Warm-Up 73
22 cars

Warm-Up 74
1. 497 students
2. 9 buses

Warm-Up 75
600 pages

Warm-Up 76
19,840 pages

Warm-Up 77
$1,198

Warm-Up 78
$342.20

Warm-Up 79
C

Warm-Up 80
D

Warm-Up 81
C

Warm-Up 82
B

Warm-Up 83
90 years

Warm-Up 84
67 years

Warm-Up 85
C

Warm-Up 86
B

Warm-Up 87
C

Warm-Up 88
A

Warm-Up 89
36 pizzas

Warm-Up 90
75 pizzas

Warm-Up 91
B

Warm-Up 92
B

Warm-Up 93
Two sides are 10 feet long, and the last side is 11 feet long.

Warm-Up 94
Two sides are 25 feet long, and the last side is 15 feet long.

Warm-Up 95
D

Warm-Up 96
C

Warm-Up 97
D

Warm-Up 98
D

Warm-Up 99
football

Warm-Up 100
They are usually fatter at the poles and rounder at the equator than perfect spheres. They also have high and low areas (mountains and valleys).

Warm-Up 101
1. 240 feet
2. 3,600 square feet

Warm-Up 102
1. 360 feet
2. 8,100 square feet

Warm-Up 103
1. 80 feet
2. 391 square feet

Warm-Up 104
1. 78 feet
2. 360 square feet

Warm-Up 105
9 inches

Warm-Up 106
10 squares

Warm-Up 107
240 cm

Warm-Up 108
432 cm

Warm-Up 109
1. 800 square inches
2. 400 blocks

Warm-Up 110
1. 9,800 square inches
2. 4,900 blocks

Warm-Up 111
1. 6 faces
2. 8 vertices
3. 12 edges

Warm-Up 112
6 cubic inches

Warm-Up 113
all but the square

Warm-Up 114
B

Warm-Up 115
64 cubic centimeters

Warm-Up 116
1. 1,024 cubic cm
2. 16 pieces of cake

Warm-Up 117
rhombus

Warm-Up 118
trapezoid

Warm-Up 119
4 inches

Warm-Up 120
1. no
2. no

Warm-Up 121
three (1" x 5"; 2" x 4"; 3" x 3")

Warm-Up 122
1. four (1" x 8"; 2" x 7"; 3" x 6"; 4" x 5")
2. Accept appropriate answers. Examples include: 6" x 6" x 6"; 5" x 6" x 7"; 8" x 6" x 4"; 8" x 8" x 2"; 8" x 7" x 3"; etc.

Warm-Up 123
Rectangle 1: 6" x 6"
Rectangle 2: 9" x 4"
Rectangle 3: 3" x 12"
Rectangle 4: 2" x 18"
Rectangle 5: 1" x 36"

Warm-Up 124
Rectangle 1: 6" x 8"
Rectangle 2: 4" x 12"
Rectangle 3: 2" x 24"
Rectangle 4: 3" x 16"
Rectangle 5: 1" x 48"

Warm-Up 125

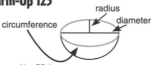

Warm-Up 126
1. diameter (twice as long as radius)
2. circumference (about three times as long as diameter)

Warm-Up 127
198 tiles

Warm-Up 128
1. 100 square feet
2. 400 square feet

Warm-Up 129
60 square feet

Warm-Up 130
105 square feet

Warm-Up 131
Answers will vary.

Warm-Up 132
Answers will vary.

Warm-Up 133
Answers will vary.

Warm-Up 134
Answers will vary.

Warm-Up 135
Answers will vary.

Warm-Up 136
Answers will vary.

Warm-Up 137
Answers will vary.

Warm-Up 138
Answers will vary.

Warm-Up 139
Answers will vary.

Warm-Up 140
Answers will vary.

Warm-Up 141
Answers will vary.

Warm-Up 142
Answers will vary.

Warm-Up 143
Answers will vary. Examples include milk, juice, soft drinks, house cleaners, etc.

Warm-Up 144
Answers will vary. Examples include gasoline, kerosene, water, milk, etc.

Warm-Up 145
9

Warm-Up 146
1. Page A = 4 stamps; Page B = 3 stamps; Page C = 6 stamps
2. Page C

Warm-Up 147
1. [10 ft.] 6 ft.
2. perimeter = 32 feet
3. area = 60 square feet

Warm-Up 148
1. P = 2 l + 2 w or
   P = 2 (l + w)
2. A = l x w

Warm-Up 149
1. no
2. The scroll is 2 feet short.

Warm-Up 150
1. 108 square feet
2. He needs 8 square feet more.

Warm-Up 151
1. 70 degrees
2. Accept appropriate answers (e.g., spring, mid day, temperate climate)

Warm-Up 152
1. B
2. B
3. C

Warm-Up 153
1. obtuse angle
2. straight angle

Warm-Up 154
Answers will vary.

Warm-Up 155
Answers will vary.

Warm-Up 156
Answers will vary.

Warm-Up 157
1. 8
2. 4
3. 4

Warm-Up 158
1. 4
2. 16
3. 128

Warm-Up 159
1. Most friends are between 9 years 1 month and 9 years 4 months.
2. 9 years 1 month, 9 years 3 months, and 9 years 4 months
3. 9 years 5 months and 9 years 7 months

Warm-Up 160
Answers will vary.

Warm-Up 161
1. between 3 ft., 11 in. and 4 ft. 3 in.
2. 4 boys
3. 11 boys

Warm-Up 162
Answers will vary.

Warm-Up 163
1. 7
2. 33%
3. 30½ days

Warm-Up 164
1. April
2. July; it is the midpoint of the year.
3. September 2 is the 245th day of the year.

Warm-Up 165
191 days

Warm-Up 166
1. 22 books
2. 11 days

Warm-Up 167
1. 3 hrs.
2. 2 hrs. and 55 min.
3. 5 hrs. and 55 min.
4. 355 minutes
5. 21,300 seconds

Warm-Up 168
1. 3 hrs. 45 min.
2. 225 minutes
3. 13,500 seconds

Warm-Up 169
1. 9 hours, 15 minutes
2. about 46 hours

Warm-Up 170
1. 5 hours, 30 minutes
2. 40 minutes
3. 4 hours

Warm-Up 171
1. basketball and football
2. 85 students

Warm-Up 172
1. football
2. 17 times
3. 118 students

Warm-Up 173
1. Crazy Legs and Big Mike's
2. Freaky Fries and Hotdog Heaven
3. 39 students

Warm-Up 174
1. Crazy Legs, Big Mike's, and a tie between Simple Sam's and The Nutty Burger
2. Freaky Fries and Hotdog Heaven
3. 91 students

Warm-Up 175
1. 4%
2. pizza
3. chicken tenders and corn dogs
4. grilled cheese

Warm-Up 176

1. Tuesday
2. Friday
3. 22%

Warm-Up 177

1. 1, 1, 2, 2, 3, 3, 4, 5, 6, 6, 6
2. mode = 6
3. median = 3

Warm-Up 178

1. 3, 4, 5, 6, 7, 7, 7, 9, 12
2. mode = 7
3. median = 7

Warm-Up 179

1. B
2. A

Warm-Up 180

1. C
2. 75%

Warm-Up 181

1. mode = 33
2. median = 29
3. range = 30

Warm-Up 182

1. mode = 36
2. median = 36
3. range = 24

Warm-Up 183

1. 16 combinations (red blouse with each of 4 shorts, yellow pullover with each of 4 shorts, blue blouse with each of 4 shorts, and purple pullover with each of 4 shorts)

Warm-Up 184

2. 24 combinations (blue shorts with each of 4 shirts, blue skirt with each of 4 shirts, black shorts with each of 4 shirts, black skirt with each of 4 shirts, khaki shorts with each of 4 shirts, khaki skirt with each of 4 shirts)

Warm-Up 185

A

Warm-Up 186

1. About 10 would be heads, because the probability is 1 in 2.
2. Over many coin flips, such as 100, the probability of 50% is more likely to occur.
3. The denomination of the coin would not matter.

Warm-Up 187

6 different ways

Warm-Up 188

24 different ways

Warm-Up 189

1. USC (3 shirts)
2. UCLA (19 shirts)
3. UND (5 shirts)
4. 6th grade (19 shirts)

Warm-Up 190

Answers will vary.

Warm-Up 191

1. 3 and 6
2. 1 and 4
3. The probability of rolling any number on a die is 1 in 6 because there are six sides with an even chance of being rolled.

Warm-Up 192

1. 2 (1 combination: 1 + 1); 3 (2 combinations: 1 + 2, 2 + 1); 4 (3 combinations: 1 + 3, 2 + 2, 3 + 1); 5 (4 combinations: 4 + 1, 3 + 2, 2 + 3, 1 + 4); 6 (5 combinations: 5 + 1, 4 + 2, 3 + 3, 2 + 4, 1 + 5); 7 (6 combinations: 6 + 1, 5 + 2, 4 + 3, 3 + 4, 2 + 5, 1 + 6); 8 (5 combinations: 6 + 2, 5 + 3, 4 + 4, 3 + 5, 2 + 6); 9 (4 combinations: 6 + 3, 5 + 4, 4 + 5, 3 + 6); 10 (3 combinations: 6 + 4, 5 + 5, 4 + 6); 11 (2 combinations: 6 + 5, 5 + 6); 12 (1 combination: 6 + 6)
2. 7

Warm-Up 193

1. 1 in 12
2. 2 in 12 (1 in 6)
3. 10 in 12 (5 in 6)

Warm-Up 194

1. 3/12 or 1/4
2. 9/12 or 3/4

Warm-Up 195

1. *TV Now* and *Sports Hub*
2. *Golf Today* and *Your Style*

Warm-Up 196

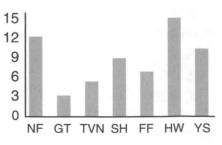

Warm-Up 197

1. 440 minutes total
2. Thursday, Saturday, and Sunday
3. Thursday and Saturday

Warm-Up 198

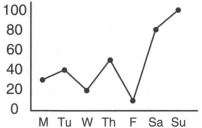

Warm-Up 199

1. 2 hours
2. Monday and Tuesday
3. 31 hours altogether

Warm-Up 200

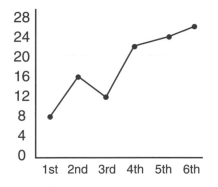

Warm-Up 201

1. sports stories
2. other
3. 30 more
4. 180 books altogether

Warm-Up 202

animal stories	⬜⬜
mysteries	⬜⬜⬜⬜
adventures	⬜⬜⬜⬜⬜⬜
sports	⬜⬜
humor (funny)	⬜⬜⬜⬜⬜
other	⬜⬜

Warm-Up 203

1. sleeping
2. watching TV
3. watching TV

Warm-Up 204

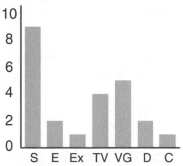

Warm-Up 205

1. Oaty Oats
2. Rice Soggies
3. 53 students
4. Oaty Oats and Crispy Corns
5. Corny Bits, Special Q, and Rice Soggies were chosen 12 times, the same as Crispy Corns.

Warm-Up 206

1. Oaty Oats
2. Rice Soggies
3. 61 second graders
4. Corny Bits was chosen half as much as Oaty Oats.

Warm-Up 207

1. 2 in 5; 40%
2. 2 in 5; 40%
3. 1 in 5; 20%
4. 4 in 5; 80%

Warm-Up 208

1. 4 in 8; 50%
2. 1 in 8; 12.5%
3. 6 in 8; 75%
4. 1 in 8; 12.5%

Warm-Up 209

1. 10
2. 35
3. 16
4. broccoli and sausage
5. 20% (7/35 or 1/5)

Warm-Up 210

Answers will vary.

Warm-Up 211

n = 42

Warm-Up 212

n = 50

Warm-Up 213

36 is greater than 5

Warm-Up 214

1. 6 is greater than 3
2. 30 is equal to 30
3. 28 is greater than 21

Warm-Up 215

4 + 3 = 7

Warm-Up 216

100/10 + 6 = 16

Warm-Up 217

t = 3

Warm-Up 218

1. n = 4
2. n = 8

Warm-Up 219

49 marbles

Warm-Up 220

12

Warm-Up 221

1.

	F	NF
M	20	10
Tu	30	15
W	18	**9**
Th	14	**7**
F	**22**	11

2. The number of fiction books is twice the number of nonfiction books.

Warm-Up 222

1.

	3rd	**4th**
Wk 1	60	67
Wk 2	77	84
Wk 3	49	56
Wk 4	76	**83**
Wk 5	63	70

2. The pattern is "+7".

Warm-Up 223

$7 + 9 = 16$

Warm-Up 224

1. Box 1: n = 5;
   Box 2: n = 9
2. Answers will vary.

Warm-Up 225

n = 11; 11 marbles

Warm-Up 226

1. $14 - 5 + 20 - 6 + 7 = n$
2. 30 marbles

Warm-Up 227

n = 90 beads

Warm-Up 228

1. $5 \times 9 \div 3 \times 20 = n$
2. n = 300 beads

Warm-Up 229

n = 9

Warm-Up 230

n = 30

Warm-Up 231

$25^2 = \$625$

Warm-Up 232

$15^2 = \$225$

Warm-Up 233

n = 19

Warm-Up 234

1. $n + 17 = 31$
2. n = 14

Warm-Up 235

$23 + 20 - 6 = 37$

Warm-Up 236

$2 (10) + 4 (5) - 5 = 35$

Warm-Up 237

$3 (12) + 5 - 6 = 35$

Warm-Up 238

$7 (10) - 12 + 4(4) - 7 = 67$

Warm-Up 239

1. C
2. Only 0, 1, and 2 added to 12 could be less than 15.

Warm-Up 240

1. D
2. Only 4, 5, and 6 added to 9 would be greater than 12. The others all had at least one number that, when added to 9, would be greater than 12.

Warm-Up 241

1. C
2. Only 4 plus 2 would be greater than 0 after 5 was subtracted. Zero cannot be greater than zero as A and B would suggest.

Warm-Up 242

1. C
2. Only $20 + 8 - 6 = 22$. All of the rest do not equal 22, as the ≠ sign says.

Warm-Up 243

s = 11

Warm-Up 244

1. $3 \times n = 60$
2. n = 20

Warm-Up 245

1. n = 84
2. $84

Warm-Up 246

1. $9 \times 8 - 13 = n$
2. $59

Warm-Up 247

1. $7 + 11 - 3 - 5 = 10$
2. $10

Warm-Up 248

$18 + 7 + 6 - 6 - 3 = \$22$

Warm-Up 249

1. 2, 5, 9, 14, 20, 27, 35, 44, 54, 65
2. The pattern is +3, +4, +5, +6, etc., with each number in the sequence.

Warm-Up 250

1. 2, 5, 11, 23, 47, 95, 191, 383, 767)
2. The pattern is "(n x 2) + 1" (multiply the previous number by 2 and add 1). Another acceptable answer is "double the number that is added."